# Finding GOD In The Fire

Tammy Lynn

Finding God in the Fire

Copyright © 2018 Tammy Lynn

Unless otherwise noted, all scripture is taken from the The Holy Bible, New King James Version. Copyright © 1982 by Thomas Nelson, Inc. Used by permission. All rights reserved.

Scripture taken from the HOLY BIBLE, NEW INTERNATIONAL VERSION®. Copyright © 1973, 1978, 1984 by International Bible Society. Used by permission by Zondervan Publishing House. All rights reserved.

The "NIV" and "New International Version" trademarks are registered in the United States Patent and Trademark Office by International Bible Society. Use of either trademark requires the permission of the International Bible Study.

Scripture quotations marked NLT are taken from the Holy Bible, New Living Translation, Copyright © 1996, 2004. Used by permission of Tyndale House Publishers, Inc., Carol Stream, Illinois 60188. All rights reserved.

Scriptures quoted from The Holy Bible, New Century Version®, Copyright © 1987, 1988, 1991 by Word Publishing, a division of Thomas Nelson, Inc. Used by permission.

Scripture taken from The Holy Bible, King James Version. Copyright © 1989 by Thomas Nelson, Inc. Used by permission. All rights reserved.

ISBN-10: 1717291767
ISBN-13: 978-1717291769

## DEDICATION

This book is dedicated to my dear sweet mother, who left this earth before any of us were ready to let her go. Thank you for teaching me how to love unconditionally, to be the type of person who puts the needs of others before my own needs, and to help those who are hurting and just need a kind word or prayer to lift them up. Thank you for all you sacrificed for the ones you loved. You touched lives in ways that you never knew. You are truly and dearly missed every single day but I wouldn't have asked you to stay another moment in pain knowing that you are now dancing with joy with our Savior and Lord. Until we meet again, I love you "bigga bigga bunches"!

Special thanks to Jackie and Jennifer without whom this story would never have been told. Thank you for your love and support through this process. I thank God for the wonderful, awe inspiring women He has brought into my life. You each mean so very much to me and have touched my heart in an everlasting way.

# PART 1
# MY STORY

# PART 2
# SURVIVING THE STORM

# Introduction

Hi, my name is Tammy and I am an overweight; codependent; neurotic; depressed; fearful; anxious; insecure; people pleaser; victim of sexual abuse; and I lack healthy boundaries in my life. I am not enough. I am never enough. Nothing I do is ever good enough. I have to try harder to do more, to be better, to make my husband and my family happy. I have to take care of everyone; and if they don't take care of something, then I need to step in and take care of it for them. I have to be good so others will love me and want to be around me. I am ruled by my fears and anxieties. I am extremely self-conscious and will stay at the back of the crowd to avoid awkwardness because I am always awkward around people. Fear rules my every step.

This was my mantra. This was how I saw myself. Until the day at the end of June 2017 when my life was shattered in an instant.

I would say it was the beginning of the end; but in reality, the ending began so long before that day.

This is my journey of Finding God in the Fire…...

## Saved By Grace

My entire adult life, I lived for my spouse and my children. I suddenly found myself lost, alone and broken in a strange city, hundreds of miles from home, where I literally knew no one. At the end of June 2017, my husband told me he wanted out of our marriage. I was shocked, afraid, shattered and oh so hurt and broken. I didn't even know who I was anymore. I had completely lost my identity amidst being a wife, mother, caretaker, provider, problem-solver, cook, maid, and general Jane-of-all-trades. In a single moment, I lost everything that mattered most to me and my life was turned completely upside down.

I met and started dating my husband shortly after graduating high school, when I was 18 years old. For most of the past eight years, we had lived apart due to his being moved around with his Military orders and my having difficulty finding work where he was stationed. I moved to Texas in November of 2016 to finally live with my husband and spend the rest of our lives together. I could finally live the dream of growing old with my love, or so I thought.

I gave up my job, my connections, and being near my family to be with my husband. I was excited to never miss another holiday together, to be a part of each other's lives again, and to finally focus on "us". Our children were all grown and living their own lives.

During the seven months between my move to Texas and our separation, we went through many struggles in our lives. Our adult daughter and two toddler grandchildren moved in with my husband a few months before I did and moved back to Oklahoma in March; I was struggling to find work; and we were told my husband was being medically discharged from the Army.

We were also trying to acclimate to living together again after being apart for so long. We were merely surviving, the way we had been doing for years, facing each obstacle as it came. But I always believed if we loved each other enough, we could make it through anything.

My husband had always struggled with depression and addiction and they were getting worse over time. He was fighting inner demons and withdrew emotionally more and more over the years; and between that and the years of living apart, we were extremely disconnected.

I tried to reach him for years but no matter what I did, it didn't seem to help. I just wanted to help take away the pain but I ended up taking on all the responsibilities and enabling his behaviors, which just caused us both more pain. The more I hurt, the more I withdrew behind the wall I had built and the more he shut down and pushed me away. Neither of us could reach the other.

My husband wouldn't talk to me about pretty much anything and never about his feelings. I felt isolated and hurt and I withdrew more and more inside myself and filled my time with meaningless pursuits like watching TV and playing games on my phone.

We had been together for twenty-three years when he said he was tired of hurting me and me hurting him. Because he wouldn't or couldn't communicate with me, I had no idea how I was even hurting him. I tried and tried but it was never enough. In the end, I had to admit that we were both broken and were cutting each other on the jagged edges of our broken parts. Hurt people, hurt people; and we were both hurting too much.

Suddenly the wall that was my protective barrier to pain came crashing down and all the pain it had shielded me from was washing over me in wave after wave of bone crushing pain. I felt a level of pain I had never known was possible. I could barely breathe through the pain, much less function. I could finally relate to the level of pain my husband walked around with on a daily basis and it nearly killed me. I literally just wanted to die so I would no longer feel the pain.

My whole world as I knew it came crashing down around me. Everything I had lived for was gone in a moment. My children were all grown and no longer needed me and my marriage was over. I was living in a place where I knew no one. My family was over 6 hours away. I had nothing but a new job where I worked from home and my faith in God.

As I always did when I was at my lowest point in life, I turned to God and I prayed. More to the point, I talked to God, constantly. Sometimes, literally just wailing or begging him to end it all.

The first couple of weeks the pain was so keen I thought my heart would stop beating in my chest, but there was also a numbness and a strength to get through that made it bearable. I could feel God carrying me through but I was begging daily that He would just end the pain. I felt very selfish but I kept saying, "I've done my part; I've been good; I've raised my children; I've helped others; please just let it all be over". After all, there is no pain in heaven.

I hadn't been to church in years and I hadn't been reading my bible for longer than I can remember, but I had always believed in God. My parents never went to church and I went sporadically when I was younger and had a way to go. Church always felt like an obligation, like something I "should" do to be a good person.

I never knew how to connect to God, and I certainly didn't feel any more connected by going to church. He was an enigma to me: some distant being that watched over us judging when we did wrong and willing to forgive our sins if we asked.

As my children got older, I thought of Him as more of a father and imagined Him viewing us as we view our children: watching as we make mistakes, giving us the free will to go the hard way, but welcoming us back with loving arms when we turned back to Him.

The following weeks after our separation, I felt like I could see everything more clearly. I could see all the things I should have done differently and my own issues that I had never really dealt with. I could see the struggles my husband was facing and how much pain he was dealing with on a constant basis.

There were so many thoughts whirling through my mind and memories replaying over and over in my head, that it nearly drove me mad. I had to start focusing on positive things to drive out the negatives. Everything I did before seemed so hollow and empty: watching TV, social media, playing games on my phone and being around other people hurt. They were all just empty ways to pass the time and I couldn't stand doing any of it anymore. Time was definitely not my friend. The days seemed to drag by and each moment, each breath was a challenge most days.

There were so many things that were out of my control and I couldn't do anything about, I had to focus on the things I could do. I started going for walks at a local park every morning and working out each day. I researched counseling options to deal with all of my repressed issues.

I listened to every positive, encouraging Christian book and relationship book or seminar I could find. I began looking for a church to attend because I was actively seeking God for comfort from the pain. My spirit knew what I needed even if I did not.

There was a church a few miles down the road from our house. I had passed it many times and would think, "that looks like a decent place to go", but I never took the initiative to go there. While driving to the park for my daily walk, my mind a million miles away; I ended up missing my turn and had to circle back to the park from the opposite direction.

It seemed like every block there was another church and each one I passed was like a beacon saying, "Go to church". I saw a bumper sticker on a car that read "It's all about HIM" and shortly after passed a billboard with these words in LARGE letters and the church that uses that as its motto.

"Okay Lord, I get it. It's not about me, my circumstances or my husband. It's about You and I need to go to church."

I began researching churches in the area. I visited their websites and watched their online services. God led me back to the original church I had passed every day just a few miles from our house: Grace Christian Center.

I contacted the church to see if they offered counseling and was given the number of the woman on staff who did marriage counseling. When I called, she told me she had a Thursday night women's group and asked me to come a little early to talk before class.

I went to the church service that Wednesday night and still felt disconnected and unsure if this was where I should be. I went to the Thursday night women's group and it was amazing. God knew exactly where I needed to be and was guiding my steps, even though I didn't realize it at the time. The women were all so welcoming and you could feel a peace and a special bond in the group. The words spoken that night spoke to my soul!

The group became my lifeline. I went to every church service after that and wouldn't miss a Thursday night class no matter what might come up. The group and the church were my anchor. The one constant, unmoving thing in my life. It was the only thing I had to look forward to each week.

I made three very good friends in the first few months. These were friendships like I had never really had before. In my whole adult life, I had one truly close friend and two other very good friends that I knew I could call when I needed a shoulder to cry on, but they were all back home and hundreds of miles away.

The friendships I made at Grace were at a different level. They shared their testimonies (their story of how they overcame and God's presence in their lives) with me and were wonderful sources of support during the times when I was struggling most. They helped me to find my new self and they began pulling me out of my shell and my comfort zone. They were the wise women God put in my life to help me find my way and to teach me how to grow closer to Him, along with Mrs. Jackie who led the women's group.

Grace offered Empower classes and I began signing up for all that I could, taking one or two each month. I learned so much in such a short amount of time. One of the very first Empower classes I took was called "Firm Foundations" and it taught about how Christ is the Foundation on which to build your faith and your relationship with God. The class was very good overall, especially for those who needed to really understand how to build their Christian faith on a firm foundation. But, there was one thing I was taught in this class (which was confirmed during my time at Grace) that I had never known and it really spoke to me. It changed my entire attitude about who I was in Christ.

They explained that "I am the Righteousness of God" and so are you, once you have accepted Christ into your heart, and repented of your sins. Nothing and no one can ever take that away from you. Just think about that, "I am the Righteousness of God". It's hard to feel less than, discarded, unworthy, not enough, or alone when you realize that.

I also began to look for volunteer opportunities in the church and in the local community to fill up my time. Again, I had to fill my time and thoughts with as many positive things as I could to drown out the negatives. I had way too much empty time on my hands and it left too much room for the Enemy to come in. So, I began volunteering every chance I had. I volunteered for every church activity we held. I joined another group that served food at a local mission once a month. I also signed up to volunteer at the local USO center (a not for profit organization that serves the military).

I wanted to ensure that I was only allowing positive things in to my life and not negative ones that would impede my spiritual growth. I was already broken enough. It would have been easy to jump into another relationship or to drown my sorrows in alcohol or other addictions, but that wasn't who I was and I knew that any of that would only make my situation worse in the end. I was already on the edge of the abyss, I couldn't allow anything that would push me over that edge. I was literally fighting for my life, my sanity, and without realizing it, for my soul. There was a period of time after my separation when I was battling extreme thoughts of suicide.

My attitude began to slowly change and I also started really growing spiritually during the next few months. Before I came to Grace, I never knew how to develop a relationship with God, or that He even really desired one. I felt like I was constantly in a one-way conversation with Him. I could see Him in some of the situations in my life and knew He was always there, but I didn't feel like I KNEW God.

Through most of the churches I attended, the sermons were what I would refer to as "Fire and Brimstone" sermons: all warnings about Hell, all the time. There was nothing about God being a forgiving and loving Father. It was more do right, get saved, go to Heaven; sin, do wrong, don't get saved and you will go to Hell. And no matter what you did, you were still going to be a sinner so you had to fight your sinful nature all the time.

There was no teaching about Rhema or being the "salt and light". There was nothing about having a loving Father who desires a relationship with you and for you to be loved, wholly and deeply. There was nothing about finding true peace and strength through

God. There was nothing about growing spiritually or knowing the Holy Spirit. There was no growth, only condemnation as I saw it.

To say I was confused and wandering around lost would be an understatement. I knew I had been saved and was a Christian. I tried to be good and do good things but I didn't really know what God wanted or expected from me. I am pretty smart and I had always done well at work and excelled in school, but I felt stupid when it came to the Bible. It didn't matter how many times I read it, the comprehension just wasn't there. At Grace, all of that began to change.

Don't get me wrong. It wasn't an immediate change. It was small things at first. Instead of sitting in the back, withdrawn inside myself; I began to sit closer to the front with some of my friends. At first, I would have my hands clasped together during worship (mostly because I didn't know what else to do with them and to keep myself from completely falling apart during service) but soon I was lifting my hands in worship and adding my voice to the sounds of praise being lifted to

Heaven. When someone asked how I was, I would say that "I'm okay, but I'm working on it".

Soon, however, my answer became "I am blessed" or "God is working all things out for my good". Instead of saying I was miserable or deeply hurting, I would say "I have turned my thoughts and circumstances over to God and He has a plan. I don't know what it is, but I trust that He has me in the palm of His hands and there is nowhere better for me to be". I would often say that "I was undergoing a Supernatural Makeover".

That doesn't mean that I suddenly didn't feel the pain anymore or that I was no longer hurting. I was still crushed and struggled to make it through most days. It meant that I knew that no matter how dark things may seem, God was right beside me and had a plan for me. I knew that He would help me through, like He always has throughout my life.

I knew that whatever may happen, I was not alone and it would be okay. I didn't like it or my circumstances but I couldn't change them. God gave me the strength I needed to get through no matter how bad things became, He was my lifeline in the storm. I took each day moment by moment and then day by day.

Breathe in, breathe out, move forward….and pray…. A LOT!!!

**Psalm 37:23-24** – [23]*The Lord directs the steps of the godly. He delights in every detail of their lives.* [24]*Though they stumble, they will never fall, for the Lord holds them by the hand.* (NLT)

# Finding Peace in the Silence

Silence had always been scary to me. I was very uncomfortable with silence and suddenly I was engulfed by it. Silence represented fear, anger, hurt, rejection, abandonment, and loneliness. Silence was cold, dark and empty.

Part of the reason I began to listen to Praise and Worship music and all the self-help and positive Christian books was to drown out the oppressing silence. In the silence, I could hear my own thoughts louder than ever and they were a whirling miasma of hurt, loneliness, and an overwhelming sense of loss and rejection. I worked from home, so my house was very quiet all the time.

Every spare moment I had (and there were a lot of them at first), I read a lot of scripture, various bible studies and I listened to Godly books and videos. Several people suggested I had too many voices in my head to be able to hear God clearly, but I never really HEARD God before then and not any clearer during those times. I needed the other voices to help me through the nothingness of the silence. If something I was reading or listening to was too painful, I stopped listening to it and switched to something more affirming.

I couldn't handle any more pain. In the silence when I wasn't reading or listening to something, I was praying or talking to God. Even on my daily walks, I was talking to God and praying, if I wasn't listening to a book or music. The silence was too much to deal with.

It was especially difficult lying in bed alone at night. All the thoughts that I had held at bay all day, were crashing in and the silence was deafening. I would lie in bed and talk to God or pray until I fell asleep, often sobbing my way to slumber. Sleeping and eating were both difficult to do in the first few weeks but even after that, I would wake up several times each night and struggle with falling back to sleep.

Over time, the emptiness of the silence was transformed into peace. I found that I could handle the silence of my daily walks, just me and God and nature. I would talk to God throughout my walk and notice the wondrous creations He had made: the trees, the butterflies, the sun shining above and the gentle breeze on my face. I have always felt the closest to God surrounded by nature. Who can see the vast blue sky and not think of the wonder that God spoke it into existence? How can you see the beauty of a butterfly and not be awed by the miracle of its creation?

My fear and dread of the empty silence transformed into the ability to bask in the presence of God in the peace of the solitude. Silence didn't have to be an angry, empty thing hanging over my head. Silence could be the medium in which I could truly find God. A place where I could meet Him with no distractions, no noise; just pure simple silence and God's presence. I began to realize that God is there in the silence. I didn't have to hear Him, see Him or feel Him to know that He was there. God is everywhere and with each of us all the time. I simply had to take the time to embrace the silence instead of running from it and He would meet me there.

**Isaiah 26:3 –** *You, Lord, give true peace to those who depend on you, because they trust you.* (NCV)

## Supernatural Makeover (Phoenix Rising)

**2 Corinthians 5:17** – *Therefore if any man be in Christ, he is a new creature: old things are passed* away; behold, all things are become new. (KJV)

Throughout this time, I began to think of myself as a Phoenix and the scripture about "beauty from ashes" often came to mind. A Phoenix was a mythical creature (in Greek mythology) that lives its life, dies by pretty much self-combusting into flames and then is reborn from the ashes. I would imagine the process is painful much like our transformation through the trials and tribulations of life, but the Phoenix rises from the ashes as a beautiful, stronger, new creature.

Sometimes our old self or circumstances must be completely burned away for us to leave them behind. We are made stronger and more beautiful once we come through the other side and rise, like a Phoenix, from the ashes.

Just like the phoenix was reborn from the ashes, we are reborn in Christ. Birth is almost always painful and often leaves scars and the same is true of our journey to become our new selves. We will often feel the growing pains of trying to let go of the old and getting used to our new being.

**Isaiah 61:3** – *To appoint unto them that mourn in Zion, to give unto them beauty for ashes, the oil of joy for mourning, the garment of praise for the spirit of heaviness; that they might be called trees of righteousness, the planting of the Lord, that he might be glorified.* (KJV)

Just like the phoenix was reborn from the ashes, we are reborn in Christ. Birth is almost always painful and often leaves scars and the same is true of our journey to become our new selves. We will often feel the growing pains of trying to let go of the old and getting used to our new being.

When a babe is thrust into the world, I am sure that it would prefer to stay in the comfort, safety and warmth of its mother's womb. But it wouldn't be good for it or its surroundings for the babe to stay where it was beyond the set time. It has outgrown its circumstances.

The same is true for us. When we are pushed into a new season in life, it is often because we have outgrown our old circumstances or it is no longer good for us there. To have a new, more abundant life; we must push into the new season and live the life that awaits us there.

**1 Corinthians 3:13** – *his work will be shown for what it is, because the Day will bring it to light. It will be revealed with fire, and the fire will test the quality of each man's work.* (NIV)

It is easy to bemoan the fires of life, but God uses them to purify us, to test the quality of our work and our life, and to show the truth by burning away the false. These times are used to strengthen us and to burn away the impurities in our lives. In a similar way, impurities are removed from refined metals through fire. The end result is a stronger and purer form of metal which has become hardened or strengthened by the fire. Think about how a farmer will burn a field in order to add nutrients for the new crops to grow and to destroy the remnants of the old crop. Once you have survived the fire, you will be a stronger and better you.

**Isaiah 48:10** – *See, I have refined you, though not as silver; I have tested you in the furnace of affliction.* (NIV)

**Psalm 66:10** – *For you, O God, tested us; you refined us like silver.* (NIV)

**Job 23:10** – *But He knows the way that I take; when He has tested me, I shall come forth as gold.* (NKJV)

I often would think about how a caterpillar becomes a butterfly. The transformation process itself is pretty gruesome and takes a lot of hard work and dedication. The caterpillar first has to spin a cocoon for itself, then it's old form is pretty much disintegrated away and regenerated into a beautiful butterfly. Over time, it was transformed, through this process, into a wondrous new creation that can fly. I can't wait to become the butterfly and fly!

**Psalm 126:5** – *Those who sow in tears shall reap in joy.* (NKJV)

**Isaiah 25:8** – *He will swallow up death forever, and the Lord God will wipe away tears from all faces; the rebuke of His people He will take away from all the earth; For the Lord has spoken.* (NKJV)

# Mercy Me

**Psalm 23:6** – *Surely goodness and mercy shall follow me all the days of my life; and I will dwell in the house of the Lord Forever.* (NKJV)

One of the first studies we did in our Thursday night women's group was on Spiritual Gifts. We each took a Spiritual Gift's Assessment and then Mrs. Jackie assigned each of us one of our Gifts to research and discuss with the group.

My top five Spiritual Gifts were Service, Mercy, Helps, Giving, and Faith. Most of these were not really a surprise to me. I have always gravitated towards helping others, even to the point of getting myself into trouble sometimes. Being of service to others and giving, got that. My faith was something I never doubted (except maybe in myself). But mercy?

Mercy was a word like grace to me. It was something of God, not something I have. Mercy, like grace, has always been one of those known characteristics of our loving God, the Father. How could Mercy be a Spiritual Gift and how could it be MY Spiritual Gift?

Mercy is defined as "compassion or forbearance

shown especially to an offender or to one subject to one's power; lenient or compassionate treatment", "a blessing that is an act of divine favor or compassion" and "compassionate treatment of those in distress", as defined by Webster.

As I researched the Spiritual Gift of Mercy, I began to see how this gift applied to me and how it made up so much of who I was and my personality. I have always been drawn to those who were hurting and wanted to ease their suffering. I have never wanted to see anyone or anything hurt or harmed in any way. Even as a little girl, I disliked seeing my siblings being punished and would want to take the pain away. A merciful person is often empathetic to the feelings and sufferings of others, deeply loyal, and shows compassionate kindness to those others may ignore.

It also gave me a better understanding of some of my more serious character flaws. A person with the Gift of Mercy needs to be needed and when they do not have others' hurts to focus on, they will become overly focused on their own hurts and pains. A merciful person may be indecisive as they do not want to cause distress to anyone through their decisions or actions and may avoid conflict of any kind.

Often a merciful person will become an enabler, develop a poor self-image, and tends to be prone to worry. All these negative aspects of the Gift of Mercy were very true about my own character. I suddenly had a deeper understanding about why I was the way I was. I had never tried to develop my Spiritual Gifts and by not using the gift, it was left open for the Enemy to exploit it and use it against me.

## Growth Through Grace

**1 Peter 2:2-3** – *²as newborn babes, desire the pure milk of the word, that you may grow thereby, ³if indeed you have tasted that the Lord is gracious.* (NKJV)

Over the next few months at Grace, I grew more and more spiritually. There was a woman in our group who was an Evangelist and acted as a Prayer Intercessor for our group. Again, none of this was familiar to me, but I felt like my husband and I really needed prayer and she was the one everyone called on to pray for them, so why not?

Even though it was difficult for me to ask anything of others, I stopped her one evening after class and asked her to pray for my husband and his situation. As we talked for a few minutes she told me, I was the one who needed prayers. She invited me to her house and we discussed my situation and my brokenness. She prayed with me and offered to mentor me in developing my relationship with God.

As we talked, she gave me several bible scriptures to write down on index cards and to speak over my life and my husband's life. She told me to make sure I implemented the scripture in my prayers. She loaned me a bible study and a devotional and told me to read them daily. She told me to hang the index cards on my bathroom mirror and to read them every day (or multiple times a day).

I bought a box and more index cards and began writing scriptures on the cards that really spoke to me. I separated them by subject: Faith, Healing, Hope, Love, etc. Whenever I needed comfort or guidance on a subject, I would pull out my scripture cards.

Erica became one of my closest friends after that night. We were both able to be a strong support system for each other in our times of need. It made me feel good to be able to give back something in our friendship. God used Erica to strengthen me and for me to soften her. We were both very opposite people but were able to build one another up as Sisters in Christ should be able to do. When I was really struggling, I would call Erica and she would pray with me about whatever difficulty I was facing.

Through my friendships with the women in our Bible Study, attending the various services and sermons at Grace, reading and listening to Christian books, going to classes that built on my Biblical knowledge, and through spending time daily with God in His Word and in prayer; my spiritual growth advanced quickly. There was still a great deal to learn, but I was growing where I was planted and nourishing my spiritual growth with as much Godly nutrients as I could.

**Hebrews 5:13** – *For everyone who partakes only of milk is unskilled in the word of righteousness, for he is a babe.* (NKJV)

# I Surrender All

From the end of June to the beginning of August, my husband and I still lived in the same house, but we were living separate lives. It was the darkest days of my life. Having him so near yet so far away was torture. Most days it all just seemed so surreal and I wasn't sure how to behave around him.

We were both trying to figure things out but knew we could never go back to the way things were. I never really drank but my husband drank quite a bit. I would maybe have one or two drinks a year, if that. But during those darkest days right after my husband told me he wanted out of the marriage, I tried to be who I thought he wanted me to be and that included drinking heavily on a few occasions.

It made me feel freer but it didn't lessen the pain. My body felt numb but my heart was still broken. On one night of extreme self-pity, I got very drunk on moonshine and was very hurt by something my husband did, so he left. My nineteen-year-old son was visiting us that night and was caught in the backlash of my pain. I had a melt down and was sobbing uncontrollably. I behaved very childishly, but I didn't care. I just wanted the pain to stop.

I tried to eat poison and began playing with any sharp object I could find. My son called my husband, and he came back in the early hours of the morning. When he got home, I was laying in the back-yard crying hysterically, begging God to take my life.

My husband was carrying his knife in a sheaf at his side and his .44 tucked into the back of his jeans. He came over to me and was holding me while I cried. While he was holding me, I saw his knife and grabbed it before he could stop me. I tried pushing it into my chest but couldn't get it in and he wrestled with me and pulled it out of my hands. I was holding the blade between my hands to keep him from taking it. It should have cut me, but it didn't.

I said something about being tired of having to be the good one, which hurt him badly, and he left me sitting in the yard and walked up to the house. As I was sitting there, I could see a dark shape in the grass and realized his gun had fallen in our struggle over the knife.

I had always hated his guns and would never touch it, but I suddenly wanted it with every fiber of my being. I didn't have any thoughts of using it. I just wanted it very badly. Once I picked it up, I had to get the safety off. Nothing else mattered. I just REALLY wanted to get the safety off.

I couldn't see very well in the dark but I managed to get the safety off and the gun went off. It fired into the ground and my husband came running toward me. I knew he was going to take the gun away and I didn't want to give it up, so I dove on it.

I know it was all so stupid but at that moment I wanted that gun more than anything I had ever wanted in my entire life. I may have been drunk but I was very lucid and intentional. I knew exactly what I was doing and nothing mattered in that moment but having that gun.

He wrestled the gun away from me and made me go inside and go to bed. My son was very hurt and upset by the whole ordeal. The next morning my husband told me the gun had jammed after it went off the first time; but there was a bullet in the chamber and if it hadn't jammed, it would have discharged again.

I could have shot someone when the gun went off. I could have hurt or killed my husband or son or someone in the neighborhood with the stray bullet. It should have gone off again when I dove on it, but it didn't.

It would have devastated me if I had hurt anyone in such a senseless way. But God was watching over me that night (as he had been all my life) and He kept any harm from falling upon anyone from my actions. After that night, I told God, "I don't want my life, my husband doesn't want my life, but apparently You do". I surrendered my life to God after that night and gave up trying to do anything outside the will of God.

**Deuteronomy 10:12** – *"And now, Israel, what does the Lord your God require of you, but to fear the Lord your God, to walk in all His ways and to love Him, to serve the Lord your God with all your heart and with all your soul,"* (NKJV)

# The Valley of the Shadow of Death

**Psalm 23:4 -** *Yea, though I walk through the valley of the shadow of death, I will fear no evil; for You are with me; Your rod and staff, they comfort me.* (NKJV)

It is easy to misconstrue this passage, but the "valley of the shadow of death" doesn't mean that you are dying. It represents going through the darkest times in your life. We have all walked through the valley of the shadow of death at one time or another in our lives. One of mine was during this period in my life.

**Job 12:22** – *He uncovers deep things out of darkness, and brings the shadow of death to light.* (NKJV)

I felt rejected, unloved, defeated, hopeless, lost, crushed emotionally and spiritually, and so very alone. It was the darkest days of my life. I was hurting more than I ever had in my entire life and all I wanted was for my husband to hold me and tell me it would all be okay. But, he didn't.

I kept hoping it was all just a terrible nightmare, and I would wake up and my life would be what it was. It wasn't perfect and it was very painful most of the time, but it was MY LIFE. I had lived years without my husband and I knew that I was happier with him than without him. I would have given anything to make my marriage work, including turning my back on God. But God wouldn't allow that.

I felt like I was walking along the edge of a cliff and it would be so easy to go over the edge. The suicidal thoughts didn't go away for several weeks (and would come back sporadically after that), and I REALLY did not want to live this life any more.

At the beginning of August, my husband moved out. His stuff was still at the house except most of his clothes. The second week of August, I was sent on my first trip for work. It was a few hours away and I would be gone for four days. As I was packing and loading for the trip, I kept walking past my husband's gun on the island. Each time I passed it, I had this overwhelming urge to take it with me. It took every fiber of my being to resist that temptation. I had no thoughts beyond taking it with me. I wasn't thinking "if I take it, I can end it all". I just really wanted it!

You see the enemy doesn't show you the whole plan he has for you. He just plants one little seed of dissention. One thought…"take the gun". I was a single woman traveling alone, the gun would provide protection, right?

But once I followed his whispered treachery, how easy would it have been to plant the next thought? Or for me to realize I really could end all the pain and suffering with one small squeeze of the trigger?

I have always HATED his guns. He took them everywhere with us, and it made me very anxious. Guns scared me. There is absolutely no situation where I would ever be willing to use a gun. Their only purpose, in my mind, was to inflict harm. I don't have anything against anyone owning a gun. That is their right. It's just not for me.

Remember, I was ruled by my fears and always imagined the worst-case scenario. But after my life fell apart, it didn't scare me anymore. I didn't really have any boundaries during that time, and I didn't really care what might happen. Outcomes didn't matter because I didn't care about the future. It was taking all my energy to survive each moment.

The days while I was away were the darkest days. I

would go workout and swim in the hotel pool in the evenings and the whole time my thoughts were so dismal. I was begging God to take my life, to end the pain, to let it all be over almost constantly. I couldn't understand anything that was happening in my life or how it had all suddenly gone so horribly wrong. How had I failed? How had we ended up here?

I can promise you that if I had taken the gun with me, I wouldn't have come back from that trip. Driving across a bridge on the way, the temptation to just drive over the edge was almost more than I could bear. Swimming made me think about how easy it would be to just sink to the bottom and let go. Death is easy. Life is hard. Dying is a little harder, especially if it isn't the Will of God.

You see when I was 15 years old, I tried to end my life. I was suffering from sexual abuse at the hands of a close relative, I felt like I couldn't do anything right when it came to my mom, and I was overwhelmed with depression and the feeling of not being enough. My mom was mad about something I had or hadn't done.

During my teenage years, my mom was dealing

with her own issues: issues with my step-dad and his emotional abuse and infidelity, issues with her job, issues with family. I also believed she suspected the sexual abuse, but it was something we didn't talk about. She was a bitterly unhappy person.

During that stage of my life, my mom was hyper-critical. If I loaded the dishwasher and didn't run it, I should have. If I ran it, I shouldn't have. I felt like I was in a no-win situation. I tried to find my way out by taking every pill in the house: bottles and bottles of pills. All of my mom's prescription medications, every over the counter medicine I could find; I probably took fifty pills.

I wrote letters to my mom and my best friend and then went back to folding laundry. After I finished the laundry, I went to my room to just drift off to sleep forever. But God had a different plan.

I soon became violently ill, vomiting up everything I had taken. It didn't take long for my mom to realize something wasn't right. I kept falling asleep and she kept asking what did I take. I remember her taking me outside and throwing a five-gallon bucket of cold water in my face to wake me up, and then they took me to the emergency room.

In the emergency room, they made me drink charcoal to absorb the pills in my stomach, and they gave me medicine to make me throw up what hadn't been digested. I was lucky they didn't pump my stomach, but the charcoal was bad enough. I recovered and life went on. God's plan was not my plan.

**Jeremiah 29:11** – "*For I know the plans I have for you," declares the Lord, "plans to prosper you and not to harm you, plans to give you hope and a future".* (NIV)

# Purging the Past

**Isaiah 43:18-19** – [18]*The Lord says, "Forget what happened before, and do not think about the past.* [19]*Look at the new thing I am going to do. It is already happening. Don't you see it? I will make a road in the desert and rivers in the dry land.* (NCV)

For the first few weeks after my husband told me he wanted out of our marriage, I went through a state of self-reflection. I could suddenly see things about myself that I had been in denial about for so long. I could see every negative attribute of my personality, hear every hateful word I had ever spoken to my husband playing over and over in my mind, and I realized how many repressed issues I had never dealt with in my life.

Every hurt was stuffed behind the wall in my mind where I simply didn't think about it. This wall allowed me to live my life without dealing with the hurts that were blocked behind it. I was very emotionally repressed. However, that wall had recently been demolished to smithereens by my husband's announcement. I still couldn't understand how we had ended up where we were but I could see many of the wrong turns I had made in our relationship and in my life as a whole.

My father died when I was five years old and I was very much a Daddy's girl. However, I could not remember anything about him or about my life before he died. What little information I knew, came from stories others told me. You see, the foundation for the wall I had erected in my mind started with the first traumatic loss in my life: the death of my father.

I only had two very clear memories and they were of the night he died and the day my mom took me to the funeral home to see him. I wasn't allowed to attend the funeral because she thought it would be too traumatic for a five-year-old. I remember thinking that wasn't my daddy in the casket; he didn't look like my daddy.

He was too yellow and dressed up, not in his normal t-shirt and jeans. It felt like that was a stranger laying there in that coffin not the loving father I adored. But I also remember now that my dad made me promise I wouldn't cry because my mom needed me to be strong for her. So, I didn't cry and the first brick in the wall was laid.

My father had many heart attacks over the years and

was in the hospital waiting to have a triple bi-pass surgery on his heart when he passed. He knew he was going to die before anyone else did. He did what he could to provide for my mom and I before he passed, and he pushed us both to be strong because he knew we would be living our lives without him.

While many more bricks in the wall were added over the years, another major addition was added in my teenage years. When I was a teenager, I was molested by a close family member. I was old enough to know better and I should have told someone. But who would I have told? I should have been able to stop it from happening, but I allowed it to happen. I let him do the things to me that he did. That was a shame that I carried around most of my life, even though the shame was his and not mine to carry.

As an adult, he would still say inappropriate things to me or try to grab at me but I just stayed out of arms reach. During this broken time in my life, I decided I wouldn't let anyone hurt me anymore with the things they said and did. By the time I was an adult, the wall was very solid and my hurts were all dammed up securely behind it. It wasn't healed, I was repressed. I began avoiding anything that would cause pain.

Before I moved to Texas, I had taken care of my mom

and my step-dad for several years. My step-dad loved me but he was an angry person and difficult to be around. He would say hateful things to me or ignore us when we went to visit if he felt upset that we didn't visit more often or because we left him in the nursing home.

After moving to Texas, I realized that he was not my burden to carry any more and certainly not alone. My mom was living in an apartment of her own and he was in a nursing home. I didn't have to deal with him unless I chose to. I had done everything I could for him for many years, it was time to let the past go.

During my few months of counseling, I began talking about my past and my marriage. I realized that I had some very deep hurts that I had never dealt with. The counselor wanted me to talk to my mom about the sexual abuse, but I couldn't see what good it would do to tell her.

I have always believed that she knew, but we never discussed it. My mom never wanted to talk about anything that was deeply painful for her. I couldn't see how telling her would do anything but cause her more pain, and she had experienced enough pain in her life. I didn't want to cause her any pain.

But I also needed to purge my own pain and shame. Holding on to it was like holding on to a poisonous thought that would keep invading my thoughts with shame and feelings of not being good enough. I sat down and wrote a letter to my mom about everything and how I felt like she should have protected me, she should have known. I wrote about the shame and how I never felt good enough or loved enough and every other hurt that I couldn't verbalize to her. I wrote it all down.

I prayed over the letter asking God to remove every hurt and sorrow that was wrapped up in those words. I prayed for forgiveness and for the ability to forgive and to let go; to no longer be held prisoner by the past. Then I went outside and burned the letter. Or at least I tried to.

It was pouring down rain and I couldn't get it to burn. But one way or another I was going to keep lighting it until it was nothing but ash. The words were washed away in the rain and the paper became a charred pile of ash before I was done. My tears mingled with the rain but I felt such a sense of peace after it was done and I felt as if a huge weight had been lifted from my soul.

I also wrote a letter to my husband, pouring out all the pain, regrets, disappointments, lost hopes and dreams. Everything I couldn't say to him, I wrote in that letter. It helped me to put it all down on paper and to get it out, to not just hold it in. I had become very resentful over some aspects of our marriage and was wrapped up in negativity. I needed to unload that emotional baggage and turn it over to God. So, I did.

I prayed over the letter and burned it alongside the one to my mom. That doesn't mean the past was completely forgotten but it didn't have the power over me that it had before. I was able to move forward with my life, growing and healing with God by my side. When thoughts would invade my mind about past issues, I would intentionally turn them over to God. I wouldn't allow them to take up root in my mind again.

**Psalm 55:22** – *Cast your burden on the Lord, and He shall sustain you; He shall never permit the righteous to be moved.* (NKJV)

**Isaiah 38:17** – *Surely it was for my benefit that I suffered such anguish. In Your love You kept me from the pit of destruction; You have put all my sins behind Your back.* (NIV)

# God of Healing

**Jeremiah 33:6 –** *"But then I will bring health and healing to the people there. I will heal them and let them enjoy great peace and safety."* (NCV)

God is Jehovah Rapha (the Lord That Heals) and He began healing me as soon as my world crumbled. I was severely overweight, weighing nearly two hundred and fifty pounds (at five feet three inches) when my husband and I separated. I had suffered from chronic headaches, migraines, and very high blood pressure for years.

My normal blood pressure level was usually around 170/135 (stroke level) and that was with taking blood pressure medicine. There were times when I would feel like my heart was going to beat out of my chest. Before moving to Texas, I had been diagnosed with a fatty liver and border line high cholesterol. My blood sugar was pushing 100 which was the high side of normal.

But two weeks after my husband's announcement, I went to my first doctor's appointment in Texas. My blood pressure was normal (135/72) for the first time in years. During one of the most stressful and hurtful times of my life, my blood pressure was normal.

In the natural it should have been through the roof, but it wasn't. They drew blood and all the test results were in the normal range. No more fatty liver, no more high cholesterol, no more high blood pressure. I was still taking the same blood pressure medicine I had been taking for years, but now my blood pressure reading remained in the normal range.

My weight was always on my mind. My husband never seemed to mind or even notice. He never said anything negative to me about my weight. But it bothered me. I wouldn't do a lot of activities with my husband and children because I would worry I was too fat to do it. "I'm too fat to fit in that", "It will break under my weight", or "I won't be able to keep up with them. I'll just slow them down" were the types of things that would always run through my mind.

I had a passionate love for chocolate and a giant sweet tooth. I didn't eat extremely unhealthy but I did drink a lot of soda. I had always struggled with my weight and it only became harder over the years. Things that worked for other people didn't work for me. I tried nearly every diet available. I ate healthier, counted calories, took diet supplements; but nothing helped. I was almost hospitalized from a bad reaction to a diet supplement even. But I still couldn't lose the weight.

**Psalm 30:2** – *O Lord my God, I cried out to You, and You healed me.* (NKJV)

After our separation, God gave me the strength to not eat the same way as before. Food didn't really matter because nothing really mattered, but I didn't crave chocolate or soda or other junk foods like I did before. I had a strength of will that had always been missing. I ate less, I walked almost every day, and I drank a ton of water.

By the end of 2017 (in six months), I had lost fifty pounds. I wasn't doing vigorous exercise or extreme dieting. I was doing the same things I had always done except I walked more and I didn't focus so much on food. I ate healthier just because it sounded better. If I ate anything too greasy, it began to upset my stomach.

God provided what I needed to be a healthier me. He was healing me from the inside out: my heart, my spirit, and my body. God's healing starts on the inside. He knows our deepest wounds are in our soul and in our heart and before we can physically heal, we need to emotionally and spiritually heal as well. I had faith that God would heal me. It would take time, but I would be fully healed and restored regardless of how things might feel or look in the natural.

**Jeremiah 30:17** – "*But I restore you to health and heal your wounds," declares the Lord, "because you are called an outcast, Zion for whom no one cares.*" (NIV)

## Finding God in the Fire

**Daniel 3:17** – *If that is the case, our God whom we serve is able to deliver us from the burning fiery furnace, and He will deliver us from your hand, O king.* (NKJV)

**Daniel 3:25** – *"Look!", he answered, "I see four men loose, walking in the midst of the fire; and they are not hurt, and the form of the fourth is like the Son of God."* (NKJV)

My mother's name was Joyce, but she was called Jo by most of her family and friends. Our relationship had many ups and downs over the years but we were very close in the end. My father died when I was five and my mom was left raising me and my four siblings from her first marriage on her own.

She grew up in a one room clapboard house in a small town in Oklahoma with her four younger siblings, her father, and her grandmother. Her mother had tuberculosis and was institutionalized while my mom was young and never came home after she was released from the institution. A few years after her mother left, her father remarried and her step-mother helped raise the family.

My mom fell when she was a toddler (doing something she shouldn't have been doing) and the fall resulted in a hernia that left her unable to do some of the outside chores or any heavy lifting. She later had surgery to remove the hernia. When she was thirteen, she contracted polio and was unable to walk from the pain. She would scoot around on her bottom to get from room to room, but she healed in time with no lasting effects from the disease. She was the strongest person I have ever known and overcame great obstacles in her life, even from a young age.

My mother worked most of her life as either a waitress or a cook. She didn't drive which left her dependent on others to go to the store or to the doctor or anywhere else for that matter. She had a couple of car accidents when she was younger and it left her with a paralyzing fear of driving. She would completely freeze up when put behind the wheel of a car.

When my father died, my mom raised me by herself until I was nine when she married my step-dad. She was very self-sacrificing and never really had anything for herself. She was always doing for others.

Her whole life she served other people in one capacity or another and she never really lived for herself. Because she was always willing to do for others, this would often leave her feeling taken for granted, unloved and resentful. She had a servant's heart but she wasn't feeling loved in return.

I never knew my mother's religious beliefs because we didn't talk about it but she never went to church that I knew of, and she never talked to me about God or praying. She went with me to a couple of Sunday school classes and service, but didn't really show any interest in it. She lived her life simply and as best as she could, doing what she felt was right.

In the summer of 2017, my mom thought she had caught a stomach bug because she was having issues with severe diarrhea. This went on for several weeks and we talked to her about going to the doctor but she felt fine otherwise and thought it would pass. She would seem to get better then have issues again over the period of about two months. It got to the point that she wouldn't want to leave the house in case she had an accident.

On September 8th, 2017; she was taken to the emergency room for severe pains in her side. My mom hadn't been sick other than the stomach issues so we thought maybe it was her gall bladder. They kept her in the hospital for pancreatitis and dehydration and continued to run other tests including an MRI.

The MRI showed a mass in her large intestine and they scheduled her for an upper and lower GI for two days later. I drove up to be with her at the hospital on Sunday, after church, because she was alone and she was very worried about the mass. I spent that afternoon at the hospital with her and went back up early Monday morning to be with her before her procedure.

They were positive it was cancer but wanted to get a better look at the tumor from the GI and take a couple of biopsies to send to pathology. That morning was the first time I talked to my mom about if she believed in God. I asked her if she was saved; and she replied, "of course", like it was silly of me to even ask. So simple and so resolute.

I asked her when she got saved and she said, "oh a long time ago, I don't remember". My mom was 76 years old at this time in her life so I imagine it was a long time ago. We talked about whether or not she prayed, and I read the "Sinners Prayer" with her.

We prayed together, and I sat by her bed reading scriptures to her while we waited for them to take her down for surgery. Mainly we focused on prayers and scripture for strength, peace, and healing. My mom has always been a worrier, but we talked about how we were going to wait until after they ran the tests and we knew what we were dealing with before we began worrying about the "what ifs". We were leaving the rest to God. We both had enough to worry about at that moment. My mom seemed at peace when they took her down and within thirty minutes, I was in the recovery room with her waiting for her to wake up.

The surgeon came in a little later and showed us the results, and they weren't good. The tumor had grown throughout her large intestine and had moved to her duodenum. It was definitely cancer, and surgery wasn't an option due to the location of the tumor. It was wrapped around the main artery that ran through her body and was involving tissue around her pancreas and liver. They had taken two biopsies and we could discuss a treatment plan once they knew what kind of cancer we were dealing with.

My mom started to cry as soon as she heard it was cancer, saying she wasn't ready to die. I told her that we were going to deal with it all one moment at a time. Right now, all we knew was that she had cancer and when we got the results back, we could deal with the next obstacle and the next decision. She took a deep breath and turned it all over to God.

I told her that if she wasn't ready to die, she needed to be ready to fight because any of the three options we were facing were going to make her very sick. The surgeon told her if she did nothing, the tumor and the cancer would continue making her very sick. If she had surgery, they would be removing most of her colon and she would need a colostomy bag the rest of her life and, it would be a very extensive surgery which would include a long road to recovery. If she underwent chemotherapy to shrink the tumor (which was his recommendation), the chemo would likely make her very sick. Any of the options were going to involve a lot of prayer and endurance on her part.

**Hebrews 10:35-36** – *[35]Therefore do not cast away your confidence, which has great reward. [36]For you have need of endurance, so that after you have done the will of God, you may receive the promise.* (NKJV)

All of this was barely two months after my whole life imploded and now we were facing another major battle. God was helping me get through my own struggles, struggles that I hadn't told anyone in my family about.

My mom didn't know my husband and I were separated. No one there did. I couldn't tell her. Telling others made it real and I wasn't ready to deal with that or to answer the questions that would invariably arise. My heart was too broken and what little strength I had left, I needed to use to be there for my mom. But when I was too broken and weak to do it on my own, I leaned in to God. I simply trusted that whatever happened, He would help us through. And He did. Not the way I wanted, but God's ways are not our ways: His are better.

The day after the biopsy, they let my mom go home. They gave her medication for the nausea and stomach issues and ordered home health care for her. My mom had just moved into an apartment of her own in an elders' apartment building in June.

Until January of 2017, she had been taking care of my invalid step-dad. He didn't want to go into a nursing home and she really didn't want him to, but taking care of him had become too much for her. He was a difficult person and didn't treat her very well, but she waited on him hand and foot. He had fallen a couple of times, and if things kept going like they were, one of them was going to get seriously hurt. We were all concerned that taking care of him was going to deteriorate her health which was still good (as far as we knew).

His going into the nursing home was a blessing in disguise. My mom was able to get her own apartment and find a true happiness and independence that she hadn't known in her entire life. We also had signed her up for assistance through the Department of Health and Human Services, which was a blessing when we found out she was sick. God was preparing the way for us, even though we couldn't see it at the time. There was no way she could have continued taking care of him once she got sick.

A month later, in early October, my mom passed away. A week after receiving her first round of chemo, she was admitted back into the hospital. She couldn't keep anything down and was too weak to do anything for herself. She was very dehydrated and her kidneys weren't functioning. When she went in the hospital, we all thought this was just the first of a series of hospital visits to come through her battle with cancer. No one thought my mom was dying. She was just very sick.

I used to tell my mom that she took care of me the first eighteen years, I've got her the last eighteen. God didn't quite give us a full eighteen, but I was able to be there for her over the past eight years when she needed me, and I was there with her at the end.

On Wednesday of that week, I had received the call that Mom was back in the hospital, while I was out of state working at a client's office. I was planning to go up and see her when I got back anyway so I decided to just go be with her at the hospital after I flew in on Friday.

When I got there, she was her normal self, with the

exception of not being able to keep anything down. They ran more tests and had put her on medication to help her kidneys to function correctly. She had no output from her kidneys and if she ate or drank anything, it would immediately come back up. By Saturday morning, she was vomiting up bile.

The doctor came in around noon on Saturday and told us that the tumor had wrapped around her bile duct and her liver was blocked and backing up, which was why she couldn't keep anything down. Her kidneys weren't reacting to the medication either. He said they could put a stint in to open the bile duct and start her on dialysis but those were really just symptoms caused by the cancer. The tumor was growing and she was too sick to do any more chemo. It was too extensive and invading too many of her organs and her major artery for surgery to be a viable option.

Mom said she didn't want to do any more procedures that would just prolong her circumstances. She agreed to do dialysis but that was all. They put a tube in to drain the bile from her stomach and a catheter to try to drain her kidneys.

I began calling our family to let them know what was going on but even at that point, we thought Mom still had at least a few weeks, not hours. That afternoon Mom's blood pressure began to drop and she was taken to ICU, only because the medicine needed to stabilize her blood pressure could only be given in the ICU. Family came in to see her throughout the day Saturday, and she visited with everyone until about nine o'clock that night. My aunt was the last one to spend time with her, and they talked about the good old days. Mom was still her normal self, sick but not dying. I think God was giving us this time to say our goodbyes, and He provided the strength and comfort we needed to get through.

She had barely slept the night before, but she slept soundly that night. She woke up around 4 am Sunday morning and asked me to pray for her and asked the nurse for some more morphine. She kept saying to just let her go to sleep, and I told her we would. I knew what she meant by the way she was saying it. She was asking me to let her go. All her vitals and everything seemed normal, but something felt off. I wanted to call my siblings, but what would I say? Nothing had changed; I just had a feeling.

A little after nine on Sunday morning, the renal doctor came in and told me that they would have to send Mom to Oklahoma City (about thirty miles away) to do the dialysis because her blood pressure was too low to do it at the hospital she was in. They needed to do the dialysis very slowly because of how low her blood pressure was already, and they were not equipped to do it there.

I knew my mom wanted us to let her go, so I talked to my brother (who my mom had made medical proxy with me the day before); and we told them not to do the dialysis. They offered to do hospice there in the hospital, and I began signing all the paperwork. Our family started flooding in to the hospital thinking they were coming to see her because she was very sick, only to get there and realize she was dying. It all happened so very fast and she passed in a matter of hours.

The doctor came around again as I was signing the hospice paperwork and the DNR. He explained that once we were ready, they would stop the medication that was keeping her blood pressure up, and she would just drift off to sleep. I called my siblings to get to the hospital as soon as they could. My brother said he couldn't be there for at least two hours, so they started another bag of medicine which would last no longer than five hours.

When the hospice nurse examined my mom to check her status, she showed me that the blood was already pulling from her legs. This was a sign that her body was already shutting down before we had even decided to let her go. My brother and aunt arrived around two that afternoon and within fifteen minutes of their arrival, Mom breathed her last and let go. It was like she was waiting for everyone to be there and then said, "Okay, I'm leaving now". In the end, if we had sent her to the City for dialysis, she would have probably passed in transit and most of the family wouldn't have been there with her.

It was so hard for me to not fight for my mom's life, but God gave me a peace about it. I could see His hands in her circumstances. The doctor had told us the day before that Mom had Stage 4 cancer, but they couldn't even tell us what type of cancer it was because the cells were all too mutated and didn't have any of the markers of their original cells. In the natural, my mom should have been sick for years and in severe pain. But we serve a supernatural God.

She was only sick for a few months and hadn't been in any real pain except the prior few days. She was able to finish out her days in the apartment that she loved surrounded by people who loved her. She left this life happy and feeling truly loved for the first time in her life. There were over twenty people in her room when she passed, with her children surrounding her and her daughter singing softly to her.

When she went in the hospital the first time, she was telling the nurses that this one person loved her or that one person loved her; but in the end, she was telling them she had five children, eighteen grand-children, and twenty great grandchildren who loved her dearly. She told me that she had been praying that she would reconcile with her brother and her son, both of whom she hadn't spoken to in some time. They each came to see her during that month before her death. I could see God working everything out. I didn't have to do anything but trust Him to take care of it, and He did.

When I had moved to Texas, I prayed that my mom would be able to finish out her days in her apartment and not have to go to a nursing home, because I knew she didn't want that. She was really happy in her apartment and in the short time she was there, the residents had all fallen in love with her. They would make her food every day when she couldn't and another one would come tuck her in at night. They made sure she was safe and taken care of.

In the natural, I should have been goo when my mom died, but I wasn't. God gave me this strength and peace that I had never felt before (or since). I didn't struggle with my mom's death. I'm not saying I wasn't sad, because I was and I still am. But God, allowed me to see that it was better for her to go. How could I possibly have asked her to stay knowing that she would continue getting worse and be suffering in pain?

God allowed me to be there with her at the end. His timing is perfect. I was able to stay by her side at the hospital, even in the ICU. Since I had just returned from a work trip, I had a suitcase full of clothes to get me through the week I was there and I was able to work from the main office in the town where my mom lived. I also happened to have two black dresses with me that I took on the trip.

I had a huge support system in Texas that was praying for me and checking on me daily. I wasn't having to face the battle alone. There was a sense of peace about it all that made it bearable. My mom had a small life insurance policy that paid for her services almost completely. We didn't have to struggle to find the money, and we were able to do exactly what she wanted. We were able to give her a beautiful but simple service, full of love and remembrance of her life and how she touched our lives.

In the end, I knew my mom was going to a better place and would never suffer again. On my way to the funeral home, I was praying deeply for God to provide the strength to endure what was to come and to provide His peace. I was praying out loud while I was driving and I noticed my seat belt light was flashing. My car makes an incessant dinging noise when I'm not wearing my seatbelt, but the entire twenty-minute trip, there was total silence. God was giving me the peace I was praying for and showing me that He was with me.

**1 John 5:14-15** – *[14]Now this is the confidence that we have in Him, that if we ask anything according to His will, He hears us. [15]And if we know that He hears us, whatever we ask, we know that we have the petitions that we have asked of Him.* (NKJV)

**Psalm 29:11** – *The Lord will give strength unto His people; the Lord will bless His people with peace.* (KJV)

## Turning Prey to Pray

**1 John 5:4** – *because everyone who is a child of God conquers the world. And this is the victory that conquers the world – our faith.* (NCV)

The week after my mother passed, I moved in to my own apartment in Texas. From the time I found out she was sick, I struggled with whether I should move back to Oklahoma to help take care of her and be there to support her. I spoke with Mrs. Jackie and my mom separately about it, and I decided to stay in Texas.

I had found a place for myself at Grace and was really growing spiritually. For the first time in my life, I had a place of my own when I moved into the apartment. I had moved directly in with my husband six months after we met (we weren't married at the time), and lived with my parents or family members prior to that. I had never really lived alone.

The prospect was both exciting and scary. I could afford it and my other bills, but just barely. It was going to be a struggle, but I was believing God would make a way. So, I took the first step to becoming my own person by getting my own place and finding myself.

The old me would have ran home as soon as I

found out my mom was sick, but I knew there really wasn't anything there for me anymore and I couldn't go back. I had to keep moving forward. When I talked to my mom about it, she told me that she really wished that I would move back but she and I both knew it wasn't good for me to be there.

I was hurting too much and when I am around my family, I gravitate towards taking care of everybody and everything. I could barely keep myself together at that point, so I really couldn't handle taking care of anyone else. I was also growing in my relationship with God in ways that I had never known how to do before. I had found a place where I could connect and grow and a support system at Grace.

The main office for my job was in the town where my mom lived, and I was very blessed to be able to work from the office whenever I needed to. I made monthly trips up to see her and be with her and worked from the office while I was there. I was able to still be a support system for my mom but not taking on all the responsibility myself. Other family members stepped in and helped her take care of things. That was good for both of us: she needed to know others loved her and were there for her, and I needed time to heal.

In November, I went to a women's retreat with church which was about two hours away. My friend and I were talking about how I had lived my whole life for my husband and children, and I didn't know what I was supposed to do anymore. She told me that I was to continue ministering to my children and grandchildren and sharing my testimony with others.

That night, part of the message was on ministering to our children and the people God brings into our lives. The message was also about forgiving and loving yourself, something I struggled with. It was confirmation of the words my friend spoke to me and God's guidance in my life.

On Sunday, Mrs. Jackie spoke. It was as if she was speaking directly to me. She spoke about the struggles so many of the women there had faced during the year and how she could feel our wounds. She said she didn't have anything that could help us, but she knew the One who does.

She talked about how she knew so many of us were

feeling overwhelmed by the trials and tribulations of our lives; that we were tired of the burdens and the struggles and the hurting; and how many of us just wanted to quit. We wanted to say, "I'm done. I can't do this anymore. I give up.".

She told us that it is not God's intent that we feel overwhelmed or burdened and weighed down. She spoke about how many times we feel like a victim instead of a victor. We often feel powerless to change our circumstances, to find our way out of the situation, and we feel out of control. When we feel powerless, our speech and our actions represent that.

We make defeated statements like "I'll try harder to do better", "I can't do anything about that", and "all I can do is pray". When you say, "ALL I can do is pray", you are saying it is a last resort, not the first and best option. God wants to come first…always. He wants us to turn ALL of our circumstances over to Him, especially our broken parts. He is where we find the power, strength, healing, and peace. We cannot do it on our own. He does amazing things with broken people. Just look at all the examples in the Bible.

**Romans 8:26** – *Likewise the Spirit also helps in our weaknesses. For we do not know what we should pray as we ought, but the Spirit Himself makes intercession for us with groanings which cannot be uttered.* (NKJV)

I was often not sure what to pray or even really how to pray to God. Was there a right and wrong way to pray? Through the months after I came to Grace, I learned that all that mattered was that I prayed throughout the day, keeping the connection between God and I open. Even when I felt like I was in a one-way conversation with God, I knew I had to keep praying and stay connected. I needed to continue talking to God and not allow anything to distance me from Him again.

I looked up scripture on how to pray, read books, listened to sermons, researched online and what I found was that there isn't really a specific formula for prayer. God already knew what was in my heart, my needs, and my words before they were uttered. What He desired was for me to focus on Him and to submit myself to Him and His will through prayer. I often followed the format of Jesus's words in the Lord's Prayer to guide me through how to pray: coming to God first in thanksgiving and praise, repenting from my sins and transgressions, asking for the needs of those who the Spirit has placed on my heart and then for my own needs, and yielding to God's will for my life.

**Matthew 6:9-13** – *[9]In this manner, therefore, pray: Our Father in heaven, hallowed be Your name. [10]Your kingdom come. Your will be done on earth as it is in heaven. [11]Give us this day our daily bread. [12]And forgive us our debts, as we forgive our debtors. [13]And do not lead us into temptation, but deliver us from the evil one. For Yours is the kingdom and the power and the glory forever. Amen.* (NKJV)

## Living in Limbo

By the end of 2017, I had fully dedicated my life to God. 2017 was most definitely the worse year of my life, and I was living in the promise that my latter would be greater than my former. I was determined to leave my past behind me. I was no longer the same person I was before my separation, but I was not yet the person I would become. I was no longer who I was, but I was not yet who I will be.

I was still a work in progress. I was in a season of waiting, growth, and healing. I was living in limbo. Everything that I knew about myself and my life was no longer true. Even my name felt as if it didn't belong to me. I was no longer a wife, but I was still married. I was a daughter without parents and a mother without children to care for.

I felt rejected, disposable, unloved and unwanted. I felt lost and lonely and that my whole life as I knew it was pretty much a lie. For the first time in my life, I had no one else to take care of. I was supposed to just live my life. But I didn't know how to live life for myself. That had never really been my reality. Suddenly at 42 years of age, I was supposed to figure out how to live for myself instead of for someone else. I didn't know how to do that.

So, what do you do when you don't know what to do? You give it to God because He always knows the way.

**Exodus 18:19** – *Listen now to my voice, I will give you counsel, and God will be with you: Stand before God for the people, so that you may bring the difficulties to God.* (NKJV)

I decided to use this time to get to know the Lord better so I could better understand His will for my life. Because let's face it, at this point, I had no clue. I knew that God had a plan for me, I just wasn't confident how I fit into that plan or where it would lead. I never had doubts in God, my doubts were all about me and whether or not I could get it right.

I was okay with not knowing the future but I had no hopes, no dreams, no vision for the future which left me feeling unsure of what I should be doing. Since I didn't know with certainty what to do, I stood still and embraced the fact that God was carrying me through. I didn't have to DO anything beyond living my life each day as best as I could and stay connected with God by praying my way through it and staying in the Word. I just needed to grow where I was and listen for His instruction and guidance in my life.

I began several Bible study plans and a one-year Bible and I read, I studied, and I wrote. The plans started in Genesis but where better to start than at the beginning in a new year. I didn't know what the new year would bring, but I had faith that it would be better than the previous year and that God held me in His hands.

We started the new year with a Daniel Fast at church for twenty-one days, from the first to the twenty-first. That meant basically fruits, vegetables, brown rice, and nuts; no caffeine, no sugar, no yeast, no chocolate, no yummy treats. Therefore, no coffee, no tea and no soft drinks or sweets.

Coffee was my go to morning rise and shine beverage of choice. Okay, I could do this. Food always been my source of comfort (thus why I was over-weight); but over the previous five months, God had given me a strength and will power I never had before.

As a result, I began to lose weight. I always said I had three addictions in life: my husband, an unnamed soft drink of choice, and chocolate. I was working on the first one (absence made that easier to lessen the addiction), and the other two weren't so hard to resist any more. The Daniel Fast was just another step towards making food less of a focus. I saw it as a way to align my mind, body and spirit to all be more focused on God.

I had never fasted before coming to Grace, so this was all new to me. I already was spending a lot of time in the Word and pursuing God. I didn't watch TV or get on social media because it was too hollow and too painful. I would go to the movies with my son or a friend, but even that was sometimes difficult to do.

I was still too raw and emotional and anything that would remind me of my old life was too painful. It was also difficult to sit through a movie without my mind wandering places I didn't want it to go. It was easier at home because I could just be me. If I needed to cry, I could without everyone seeing me break down. I didn't have to hold anything back when I was alone.

But I also knew I couldn't stop living life and that it is a process. Isolating myself was not going to help me to heal. I had to live my life very intentionally during this season of my life to keep from breaking apart completely. The Daniel Fast provided structure and a route to deepen my relationship with the Lord and to connect with the Holy Spirit.

**Psalm 27:14** – *Wait on the Lord, be of good courage, and He shall strengthen your heart; wait, I say, on the Lord!* (NKJV)

## Closing the Door

I still loved my husband very deeply, but I knew that if it wasn't something we both wanted; it would never work. He was living an extremely self-destructive life, one that I couldn't be a part of. I had fought for my marriage the first couple of months after he said he wanted out. I did things during that period of time that I would never have imagined I would do.

But as I said, I wasn't really myself and there were no boundaries for me for a little while. God, through the Holy Spirit, kept me from going too far off course but I was willing to live in darkness with him if that was the only way we could be together. My husband was running from the things that hurt him, and at that point, I was one of those things.

People are often drawn to the light of God within you; he was repelled by the light in me. Darkness cannot live near the light. The closer to God I became, the more he separated himself from me. In the end, I wanted his happiness more than I cared what happened to me. I was willing to go through anything for him to be okay, even if that meant letting him go.

Letting go was possibly the hardest thing I had ever had to do in my life. My heart was breaking. Each step apart was another shattered piece of my heart. You see, I truly loved my husband; more than my own existence. No matter how I might try to stop loving him, it is always there and probably always will be.

I truly believed that God made me for him. My dream was to be married for fifty years. But sometimes love alone is not enough.

These were the vows I wrote my husband on our wedding day. I remember how excited I was to finally be getting married and to live our lives together "'til death do us part".

*On this day, these are the vows I make to you,*
*To show my love is true.*
*I promise my love to you, from now until forever.*
*May our love be enough to keep us together.*
*I promise to stand by your side through the good times*
*and bad,*
*To bring you joy, when you are sad.*
*I promise to stay by your side through thick and thin.*
*I am here honey, until the very end.*
*I promise to be your friend, your wife, and your lover,*
*And to our kids, to be a good mother.*
*I promise to always be loyal, faithful, and true.*
*I promise to never lose my trust in you.*

*I promise to never let us grow apart,*
*Or let anything lessen the love for you in my heart.*
*I will give up everything I have to give,*
*As long as by your side is where I will always live.*
*When I found you, I found the other half of me.*
*Loving you is what makes my life complete.*
*I promise to never leave or turn you away.*
*By your side is where I will always stay.*
*I want us to grow old together.*
*I want us to have each other forever.*
*I want you to be my husband, and I, your wife.*
*I am asking, will you give me the rest of your life?*

But life doesn't always go the way we plan. I hadn't worn my wedding ring in many years because of the weight I had gained. I had already had it sized up once and didn't want to weaken the band by having it altered every time I gained weight. Besides, I was going to lose the weight one day.

It bothered my husband that I didn't wear my ring, but I didn't need it. Everyone around me knew I was married. I talked about my husband and my children all the time. They were my life. I was married in my heart; the ring was just an outward symbol to the world that I was married.

After the separation, I wore my wedding ring every day until the end of the first week of January. I wore it because without my husband in my life, the outward symbol was needed for the world. I wore it because I was praying God would heal my husband's heart and restore our marriage. It was an act of faith. I wore it because suddenly I needed to wear it when before it wasn't a necessity.

I was struggling with not thinking about my husband all the time and dwelling on the past. The first Sunday of January, I felt guided to take my ring off for a week to break the ties that bound my thoughts to my husband. It wasn't healthy for me to be constantly thinking about him and the past and to heal I needed to be more focused on God. The ring was a distraction and a comfort to me, a safety net of sorts.

The following day after I took off my ring, my husband told me he had started the divorce proceedings. One more door closed on the chapter of our life together. One more broken piece of my heart falling to the floor. One more step closer to God.

**Revelation 3:7** – *"Write this to the angel of the church in Philadelphia: 'This is what the One who is holy and true, who holds the key of David, says. When He opens a door, no one can close it. And when He closes it, no one can open it'"* (NCV)

## Helpless, Hopeless and Hapless

When my daughter was in her late teens and early twenties, she was always calling me when she would get into a bind or didn't know what to do. She wasn't very good at adulting and would put off things that were important and shouldn't be put off and this often resulted in compound mistakes piling up into one big mess. I would give her advice or help her out of the sticky situation as best as I could, often enabling her more in the process. I frequently teased her about being "helpless, hopeless, and hapless".

During my period of utter brokenness, those words came back to haunt me only I was the one who was helpless, hopeless and hapless.

Helpless: weak, unable to help oneself, powerless, incapacitated, or overwhelmed by an uncontrollable urge.

Hopeless: to be hopeless means one is despondent, without hope, living in despair, being unable to learn or act and possibly even incompetent at the task at hand.

Hapless: an unfortunate or unlucky person; often being pitiful, woeful and miserable.

That certainly described my situation. I couldn't control my feelings, I felt powerless in the situation I found myself in, and I felt incapable of surviving most days. I had no hope for the future or even my present life, I was very despondent, and I certainly felt incompetent to change my situation or my circumstances. I was miserable, pitiful (full of self-pity), and felt extremely unfortunate.

**Luke 1:37** – *For with God, nothing shall be impossible.* (KJV)

The good news was none of this mattered because I was not the one in control of my circumstances or my life. I might have been helpless, hopeless, and hapless on my own; but with God, nothing is impossible. I surrendered it all to God and He provided my hope, my help, and my way through the storm.

When I felt totally despondent and at my most broken, I would kneel on the floor and pray….and sob…...and pray some more. I found hope in each ray of light that God shone through the darkness surrounding me. I found help in the daily devotionals, in the Empower classes at church, in the love and encouragement my friends showed to me. I knew that I served a God that can make a way where there is no way, with whom nothing is impossible and if I kept God at the center of my life, He would take care of me and I would be okay.

**2 Corinthians 12:9** – *And He said to me, "My grace is sufficient for you, for My strength is made perfect in weakness." Therefore most gladly I will rather boast in my infirmities, that the power of Christ may rest upon me.* (NKJV)

Things may not turn out the way I wanted them to, but God would guide me and protect me, teach me the things He needed me to know and show me the way. I just had to trust in Him, do my best, and have faith that He would take care of the rest. It was easier to do at times because I felt too weak to do anything on my own. God's greatness will show out in our utter weakness. My hope was in the Lord.

**Psalm 33:20** – *We put our hope in the Lord. He is our help and our shield.* (NLT)

**Jeremiah 17:7** – *"Blessed is the man who trusts in the Lord, and whose hope is the Lord."* (NKJV)

# Breaking the Chains

**1 Corinthians 6:12 –** *"I am allowed to do all things", but all things are not good for me to do. "I am allowed to do all things," but I will not let anything make me its slave.* (NCV)

Life is about choices, but not always our own. As we ended the fast and six months had passed since my husband moved out, I was still struggling with living the life I had. I was living a life I didn't want, didn't ask for and didn't choose. My choices had contributed to the circumstances, but they were also the result of choices made by other people.

I had allowed hurt, disappointment and seeds of bitterness to grow over the years. When I reacted with unkind words, withdrawing from my spouse, silent tears, and letting other things come before God in my life; those were my choices that contributed to my circumstances. Our separation was not my choice. My husband choosing another life was not my choice. My mother's death was not my choice. But all these things, and many others, contributed to my brokenness.

Regardless of how others' choices affected my life, how I reacted to those things were my choice. I chose to live for God. I chose to love and forgive over bitterness, anger, or hate. I chose to let go and let God instead of trying to "make" things happen the way I wanted them to. I chose to go to church, to serve, to connect, to grow over sitting alone in the darkness and misery of my emotions. I chose to face the fear and walk through the fires of life over curling up in a ball and crying my life away. I chose life over death.

Sometimes, I felt like I didn't really have a choice but life is about freewill and there is always a choice to be made. I chose to not allow my life to be ruled by my emotions but by God's promises in His Word.

Because I was a merciful person, my emotions have always been a driving force in my life. But emotions are changeable and unreliable. They can be manipulated by others, the world, and by the Enemy. They can be a good thing but they can also be a major weakness.

During the darkest times, my emotions were a whirlwind of chaos threatening to swallow me whole. At the same time, I struggled with "hearing" or "feeling" God. I knew He was there and I was doing everything in my power to develop a relationship with Him, but I didn't "feel" any closer to God than before.

I understood Him better and I was growing spiritually, but I didn't feel that I was grower closer to God. Sometimes God remains silent for a reason and sometimes we have to train ourselves to "listen" for God. For me, God never really "spoke" to me.

I would sense God moving in my life by the things happening around me, things that only God could do. I would find God in His Word when certain verses or writings stood out and "spoke" to my heart. I would find Him in the many devotionals and books I read, and even the sermons at church. I would sense Him in the fresh breeze blowing on my face, in the awe-inspiring wonder of a beautiful clear blue sky. I would "hear" Him through words of confirmation spoken by others.

**John 8:47** – *He who is of God hears God's words; therefore you do not hear, because you are not of God.* (NKJV)

I believe that during this time of silence God was trying to teach me several things. First, He was teaching me to be okay in the silence. He was breaking the chains of fear. Silence is the only place to hear "the still small voice" of God. He was showing me how to tune out the distractions and white noise of life and focus on Him, fully and completely.

Second, He was teaching me to trust Him and continue walking in faith, regardless of how things may appear in the natural. I serve a super-natural God and six months to Him is nothing but a speck of dust in the wrinkle of time. He was growing my faith and reliance on Him to help me break the chains of old habits.

Third, He was stretching me. God was continually pushing me ever so gently out of my comfort zone. He was breaking the chains that bound me to where I was, to the past and to my pain. He was teaching me to stretch to make room in my life for what He had for me. If my life was already full, where would the new life He had for me fit in? He needed me to overcome my fears of the unknown and lean into Him more deeply, not on my own limited human understanding.

Fourth, He was growing the seeds in my life which had been planted and helping me to plant new seeds for fresh growth. He was weeding my garden, removing the obstacles that had kept me from being all He had called me to be. He was also pruning the good growth in my life to promote expanded growth from the strongly rooted good seeds that were already there.

Fifth, He was teaching me that my feelings were fickle but my God never is. He was showing me that He is constant and true, never changing; while my feelings and emotions, my wants and desires, were always changing. He was teaching me to allow Him to be my rock and my firm foundation, led continuously by the Holy Spirit and growing more and more Christ-like in my walk of life; rather than trying to do life on my own or in my own strength, knowledge, abilities, and understanding. We cannot live the abundant life we have been called to live on our own. It takes God to move the mountains, break the chains, and lift us up to see our higher calling.

**John 15:2** – *Every branch in Me that does not bear fruit He takes away; and every branch that bears fruit He prunes, that it may bear more fruit.* (NKJV)

**Philippians 2:13 –** *For God is working in you, giving you the desire and the power to do what pleases him.* (NLT)

# Overcoming People Pleasing

**Galatians 1:10** – *Am I now trying to win the approval of men, or of God? Or am I trying to please men? If I were still trying to please men, I would not be a servant of Christ.* (NIV)

I have spent my whole life trying to please others. I found my happiness in making others happy, which in its self is not a bad thing. The problem with my trying to make others happy was I often ended up taking on the responsibility for their happiness.

I have always hated conflict and avoided it at all cost. If someone asked me for something or to do something, I found it difficult to say no, even if I wanted to. When I did say no, I would feel guilty and would often give in and do it anyway. I wanted to please others and to feel like I was valued and loved by them.

As I said before, I lacked healthy boundaries. My best friend once told me that I was like a lonely, over-excited puppy that stood up and peed all over itself when anyone paid me any attention, especially with my family. I wanted others' approval and love so much, I was willing to sacrifice anything for them to get a crumb of affection in return. I was living a servant life but not a Godly life of service. God calls us to serve one another; but we are to do it in God's way, with His guidance on where and when to serve. It also isn't healthy to give all of yourself to anyone but God.

When your total life focus is on serving others without receiving the rejuvenation and refreshment from God, you become burnt out and resentful. My loved ones would often tell me to stop being a doormat to others, and I would just as often remark that they were one of the ones whose footprints were right there across my face. It was somewhat of a joke in our family, but was grounded in truth. During this period of brokenness, through self-preservation, I began to erect healthier boundaries and I learned the value of the word "no" in my life. I stopped giving of myself to the point of emptiness, continuously stretching myself to the point of breaking. I began to stop doing things for others if it would cause me pain or allowing the actions of others to hurt me.

I was hurting too deeply and couldn't handle anything that would cause more pain; so, if it was painful, I didn't do it. I eliminated negative habits and circumstances from my life so there would be room for the positive gifts of God and growth in my life. I intentionally removed things from my life that would come between my relationship with God and added the things that would promote my growth with God.

I began taking responsibility for my choices, my life, my actions and reactions; and I stopped taking responsibility for the choices of others, their actions or reactions. I worked on speaking positive, life affirming statements over my life and the lives of my loved ones. I would speak out loud the things I was praying for and believing God would provide. Speaking God's Word out loud against our troubles breaks the power the Enemy has on them. It covers the situation in God's light and healing. The only thing that could heal me was God, and I NEEDED healing. I overcame people pleasing by focusing on pleasing the Lord in all of my ways.

**Hebrews 4:12** – *For the word of God is living and powerful, and sharper than any two-edged sword, piercing even to the division of soul and spirit, and of joints and marrow, and is a discerner of the thoughts and intents of the heart.* (NKJV)

# I am a Palm Tree

**Jeremiah 17:8** – *For he shall be like a tree planted by the waters, which spreads out its roots by the river, and will not fear when heat comes; but its leaf will be green, and will not be anxious in the year of drought, nor will cease from yielding fruit.* (NKJV)

I had always thought my name meant "twin" but during my research for class, I realized Tammy came from Tamar in the Hebrew which means "palm tree". Our pastor ended the service at Grace most days with prayer that we "be like the tree planted by the living water".

When I realized my name meant palm tree, this really resonated with me. I had heard it said that we are often called to grow where we are planted and I felt very strongly that was the case for me in this season of my life. I came to Texas to be with my husband but once he told me he wanted out of our marriage, there really wasn't anything here for me or a reason for me to stay. But, God had me here for His own reasons. I didn't know what those reasons were, but I knew God meant for me to be here. So, I stayed and I lived my life like a Palm Tree planted by the river's waters.

In a great storm, such as a hurricane, palm trees will survive the storm while other trees are uprooted, broken, and destroyed. A palm tree will survive the storm because it is extremely flexible and it is not rigid like most other types of trees and will bend and sway with the storm instead of being snapped by its resistance to the winds. Its flexibility comes from how it is grown on the inside (made of porous, flexible material rather than stiff woody material) and from its large fibrous root system.

In the same way, we are able to survive the storms of life based on what (and Who) is on the inside of us, the One who teaches us to bend and sway with the stormy winds of life. Palm trees grow straight and tall, just like we are to grow heavenward in our Christian walk in life. They are extremely fruitful and their fruit gets sweeter as the tree ages, just as we are called to be fruitful and how as our Christian life matures, we will bear sweeter fruit. These trees survive harsh conditions, desert climates, and are often a sign of water in the dry desert to those suffering of great thirst.

Similarly, our lives as Christians are to draw non-believers to the living water and the source of life through Christ, that we may be a sign to those who are lost and guide them to the vine that offers eternal life. To live my life like a palm tree meant to grow deep roots in God's Word and in my faith that God would carry me through the storms, for me to be flexible and to not break under the strains and pressures of life; but to stand tall in my continual growth towards God and to always bear good fruit in all seasons of my life.

**Psalm 1:3** – *He shall be like a tree planted by the rivers of water, that brings forth its fruit in its season, whose leaf also shall not wither; and whatever he does shall prosper.* (NKJV)

**Psalm 92:12** – *The righteous shall flourish like the palm tree: he shall grow like a cedar in Lebanon.* (KJV)

My part of the equation was to continue believing, even when I was not seeing; to continue loving through the pain and sorrow and leaning deeper in to God, trusting Him and His ways; having faith that God would lead me and guide me through the storms when I did not have the strength to bear it on my own. I was to draw nearer to God through His Word and patiently endure the storms of life until the seas around me were overcome with His perfect peace.

I was to continuously submit myself to God and His Will and He would provide the way. To sow good fruit in my life and my relationships, I had to focus on developing the fruits of the Spirit within me: love, joy, peace, forbearance, kindness, goodness, faithfulness, gentleness, and self-control. I was to stand still and wait patiently for the Lord to direct my steps before I moved.

**Galatians 5:22-23** – *[22]But the fruit of the Spirit is love, joy, peace, longsuffering, kindness, goodness, faithfulness, [23]gentleness, self-control. Against such there is no law.* (NKJV)

**Revelation 14:12** – *This calls for patient endurance on the part of the saints who obey God's commandments and remain faithful to Jesus.* (NIV)

**Psalm 37:7** – *Be still before the Lord and wait patiently for him; do not fret when men succeed in their ways, when they carry out their wicked schemes.* (NIV)

# Be Mine

**Isaiah 43:1** – *But now, thus says the Lord, who created you, O Jacob, and He who formed you, O Israel: "Fear not, for I have redeemed you; I have called you by your name; You are Mine."* (NKJV)

After a devastating event or loss in our lives, the "firsts" are very difficult to walk through. There was the first Thanksgiving after my mom passed and my husband chose a different life. Throughout the years of my marriage, we would always go to my mom's house for Thanksgiving and then rotate the next year and go to my mother-in-law's house for Thanksgiving.

When I moved to Texas in November of 2016 (only one year prior), I remember how excited I was to be moving back in with my husband and my daughter. I intentionally made my last day at work on November 18th so I would be moved before Thanksgiving and would finally be able to spend it with my husband as we had lived in separate states most of his time in the military. I was so happy to be able to cook for my family and to celebrate the holidays with them again.

Only one short year later and I was more alone than ever. Only now I didn't even have the option of going to see my mom for the holidays. I didn't want to be around other people, and I REALLY didn't want to be around other families. It just made it all more painful to see what I had lost in the happiness and togetherness of others. So, I served.

We served Thanksgiving dinner at the local mission, where we served over eight hundred people. That afternoon and evening, I went to my friend's house and had dinner with her and another friend. No traditional Thanksgiving activities or food. Just serving and fellowshipping with others.

I had always loved Christmas and the months leading up to it. When my children were younger, we would have snack nights, read Halloween stories, watch Halloween movies and play games up until Halloween. Then we would set up the tree and decorate the house for Christmas in November. We would have family nights playing games, watching holiday movies, eating holiday treats and snacks, going to see programs or activities near us, and drive around looking at the various displays of lights. It was some of my favorite times spent with my kids when they were younger. But that first Christmas was cold, empty, dark and alone.

Everything felt so hollow. I was so very sad and broken and alone. I felt like a shattered porcelain vase that had been glued back together but would shatter again at the slightest amount of pressure. Everything hurt and being around other people made it hurt even more. I didn't decorate for any of the holidays or cook any holiday meals or do any holiday shopping. I avoided places where families would be, like the mall or any festivities. I didn't want to join any holiday activities.

I just wanted to barricade myself in my apartment and hide under my quilt my mom had made me until the new year arrived. But that wasn't realistic or healthy. If I couldn't hide from it and pretend like it didn't exist and it hurt too much to celebrate it, what could I do?

I could focus on the true meaning of Christmas and serve others through the pain. I spent Christmas Day serving at the USO so soldiers who had nowhere to go, would have a place to be on Christmas Day and so other volunteers could spend the day with their families. My youngest son spent the day with me there as well.

The Saturday before Christmas, we served a Christmas meal and gave out gifts at the local mission. We served over one thousand people that day. I served because it was better to focus on serving others than to wallow in my own self-pity and pain and let the darkness and depression overtake me. I was still devastated and deeply wounded, but I was walking through it all in faith that God would help me through. And He did. It wasn't easy, but God made it bearable.

I spent more one-on-one time with the Lord and dug deeper into the life of Christ and the first Christmas. It was the simplest and most peaceful Christmas season I had spent in many years. I had no concerns about taking care of anyone else or their needs.

I just sat in quiet communion with the Lord, and I prayed the whole painful season would pass as quickly as possible. I also prayed that whatever God needed me to learn from this season in my life, I would learn it, and that His will would be done in all things. It hurt and

I still begged God to take me home most days, but I knew I wasn't walking through it alone; that no matter how painful it was, God was there wiping away my tears and holding me through it all. Each time I felt like crumbling into a helpless mass of tears, I would pray harder and focus more and more on God until I could see my way through the haze of pain.

I continued my walk of faith through the many "firsts" in the months that followed my mother's passing and the crumbling of my marriage. The first Thanksgiving, the first Christmas, the first New Year, my first birthday and the first Valentine's Day. My birthday was at the end of January and I just wanted it to pass and to ignore it and act like it didn't exist, not because I was getting older or due to my age. I never really cared about any of that.

I wanted it to just slip quietly by and ignore it because it would be the first birthday when I wouldn't get a call from my mom telling me happy birthday. It was another day spent alone, without my husband, and feeling lonely so I wanted it to come and go, to be behind me and a part of my past. I went to Oklahoma and spent the day with my daughter and grandchildren. I was still sad but I was able to walk through it by leaning into God and focusing on Him rather than on my circumstances.

I found the month leading up to Valentine's Day more difficult than I had ever imagined. My husband and I didn't really celebrate Valentine's Day and he was never much of a gift giver, but everything I saw about Valentine's Day that year was very painful. Every store display, every commercial about celebrating with your love, the advertisements for marriage seminars and classes at church, every loving couple I saw, every red heart was a painful reminder of what I had lost.

Each painful moment was like a sharp pang in my chest, a gut clenching pain that would steal my breath away. Valentine's Day happened to fall on a Wednesday and that night during the service, I sensed God telling me to not be distracted from His love for me by the things of this world and the attacks of the Enemy. He was saying to me "Just be Mine" and the rest didn't matter. He was showing me His love through the friendships I made here and the people who messaged me that day to just say "I love you". One of my very good friends brought me flowers to show me that I am loved.

I chose to live my life for God and not for myself or for others. The blessing of being God's is that He will never abandon me; He is always there. His doors are never closed, His business will never go under, and His pay checks will never bounce. He will never give up on me regardless of who else in my life may leave me or forsake me. He promises He never will. He takes care of His children. He safeguards and protects them. He loves like no other. I didn't have to feel unloved when I lived in the love of My Heavenly Father.

Even when we are discarded by people of the world, we are treasured by our Father. It helps to get through the times of brokenness to remember that God accepts us as we are, in all of our brokenness. He is willing to heal our broken parts and make us into His masterpiece.

We just have to be willing to allow Him in to do the work. We don't have to hide anything from Him;

He already knows the truth. It wasn't easy and it was still extremely painful, but I continued walking forward in faith and trust that God would lead me through the storm and bring me out into His light and into something greater.

**Colossians 3:23** – *Whatever you do, work at it with all your heart, as working for the Lord, not for men.* (NIV)

**Psalm 37:5** – *Commit your way to the Lord, trust also in Him, and He shall bring it to pass.* (NKJV)

## This Little Light of Mine

**Ephesians 5:8** – *For you were once darkness, but now you are light in the Lord. Walk as children of light.* (NKJV)

**Genesis 1:3** – *Then God said, "Let there be light"; and there was light.* (NKJV)

I loved this song when I was a little girl: "This little light of mine, I'm gonna let it shine. Everywhere I go, I'm gonna let it shine. Out there in the dark, I'm gonna let it shine".

I have always felt like my purpose in life was to be a light to draw others closer to God, to just let my inner light shine and to help others in need, to encourage others and to show them the love of God. I often struggled with talking to people about God or my beliefs because I never wanted to seem pushy.

I never felt like I knew the Bible well enough to talk to others about it. I had my faith and my beliefs, but they were very personal for me and not easily shared. I tried to live my life as Christ-like as possible and prayed often. But I never felt connected to God other than through prayer. Church was usually very dry, and I didn't feel more connected to God by going or by reading my Bible because the revelation just wasn't there.

Part of my character was to have a naturally loving heart. I have always had so much love to give, and I was continuously seeking people to give my love to. I was soft-hearted, kind, and considerate. I enjoyed helping and serving others, and I smiled a lot (even when I did not feel like smiling). I was a natural peace maker and gravitated towards mediating in disagreements between others because I could see both sides, and I could help explain what each person was trying to say.

I had an aversion to conflict and confrontation. It made my spirit uneasy. My aunt once called me Pollyanna because I kept mentioning the "brighter" side of the circumstance. This was more difficult for me to do in my own situations than in the situations of others.

When I was younger, I was often called "Smiley" because I had a natural joy that shown through. But as often happens, life dimmed my inner light through pain, resentment, unhappiness, and brokenness. I let the darkness drown out the light much too often in my life. Each heartache and hurt dimmed my light more.

**Luke 11:36** – *"If your whole body is full of light, and none of it is dark, then you will shine bright, as when a lamp shines on you."* (NCV)

In the following months after my life collapsed, people at church would tell me I was "glowing", that they could see the joy radiating from me, or that my smile drew them to me. I thought it was funny that they could see joy in me when I was certainly not feeling very joyful.

Despite my circumstances, I could smile as I walked through it, even when I didn't feel like smiling. But I believe that what they were really seeing was the joy of the Lord shining through me. It was not my natural joy because there was no joy in my life at that time, it was the supernatural joy that God was gifting me with. The inner light He had lit inside me that would shine through to others. It drew people to me because it made them feel good.

In order to keep my light shining as brightly as possible and to not dampen or extinguish it; I had to feed it with the Word of God, fuel it with my faith that God would bring me through the tribulations I was facing, and let my prayers burn brighter for the Lord. I stoked the fire by serving others, by choosing to focus on God instead of my troubles, and by choosing forgiveness and love over bitterness and hard-heartedness. I chose the peace of the Holy Spirit, the compassion of Christ, and the love of God over any of the lies and negative emotions the Enemy was trying to plant in my heart. I chose to continue to live for God and to walk through the fire with Him by my side, regardless of the storm and fires raging around me.

**Psalm 18:28** – *For You will light my lamp; the Lord my God will enlighten my darkness.* (NKJV)

**Psalm 27:1** – *The Lord is my light and my salvation; whom shall I fear? The Lord is the strength of my life; of whom shall I be afraid?* (KJV)

# Making Peace with the Broken Pieces

**Matthew 5:9** – *God blesses those who work for peace, for they are called the children of God.* (NIV)

I am naturally a peacemaker not a troublemaker but I struggled with finding true peace in my life, especially in my darkest, most broken times. I knew to move forward, I had to find peace with myself and with where my life was. When your life is rocked in a foundation shattering way by the loss of a loved one, the collapse of a relationship or other devastating event such as a major illness; there are suddenly some broken pieces of your life that no longer fit.

A friend of mine from church lost her young son in December, and we were talking about the misfit pieces one day during a church event. We were both trying to fill out the cards where you give your basic information: name, address, marital status, number of children, etc. We looked at each other and were discussing how the simplest things suddenly became very difficult because you simply didn't know how to really answer the question and it brings a sudden stab of pain and panic.

For me, it was the question on Marital Status or Spouse's Name (options: married, single, divorced, widowed). I didn't really fit into any of those categories. I was technically still married but separated would have been the more appropriate response and if I put married, then I was supposed to list my spouse's information and there was no way I could do that.

For my friend, the broken piece was Number of Children. She put three because she HAS three children even if she is no longer able to hold one of them in her arms. Another stumbling block for us is when we had a new person at our Thursday night Women's Bible Study.

We would go around the room, each introducing ourselves and then telling the newcomer a little about ourselves. The usual answers were "I've been at Grace xx amount of time, I am married with xx number of children, etc.", but our answer before the storm was not the same as our answer in the midst of the storm.

There are so many broken pieces that no longer fit in the puzzle of life. The question I faced was: what do I do with the misfit and broken pieces of my life?

There were so many pieces of my old life that didn't really fit any more: the family pictures, the wedding photos, the letters and cards my husband and I sent to each other over the years, our wedding rings, the "memory" boxes full of sentimental items we each had saved over the years, the things that we had bought together over the years as a part of our lives together....the list goes on and on. What was I to do with all of these misfit pieces?

I was struggling with letting go of the past when I looked at these things and all the pain, sorrow and sadness would threaten to swallow me whole. Everything reminded me of my husband: every motorcycle that drove by, every white truck I saw, every restaurant I went to where we had ever shared a meal together, the songs on the radio, walking through the grocery store, driving down the road, our children and grandchildren, the myriad of posts on social media, the photos of our life together.

I couldn't escape the painful memories or thoughts. I struggled with what I should do with the physical items that embodied these memories. Should I keep them? Should I throw them away? Should I burn it all?

This was MY LIFE represented in these things. It was who we were together, the memories we shared, the love we exchanged, our family, our children and grandchildren…. our whole life as husband and wife was now packed away in boxes. I couldn't just throw it all away or pretend like it didn't happen.

It was all part of the journey through life that made me who I was (even if that was nothing but brokenness at the moment, it was ME). My husband may have thrown away our life together but I could not. I could not regret one minute of the life I lived (regardless of the tragic ending and bitter turns).

I LOVED greatly. I couldn't pretend I didn't; and if I did anything out of pain, bitterness, anger or in reaction to the circumstances or my emotions, I knew I would later regret it. I try to live my life with the least amount of regrets because I feel like it is a wasted emotion; I wasn't going to feed it by behaving in an ungodly way. But how should I deal with it in a healthy and life affirming way?

I prayed about it all. I asked God to show me what

to do with the misfit pieces, and I recognized that it was part of the process. Those difficult things we don't want to deal with are a playground for the Enemy to use as stumbling blocks in our growth, healing, and forward momentum. He uses them to kill our joy, steal our peace, and destroy our progress.

I went through my old journals (spanning various periods over the past 10 years); and I tried not to relive the feelings or bitterness but to look at the truth through a Godly lens. If something I wrote caused me pain, I would pray about it and ask God to remove "any hurt, bitterness, resentment, anger or negative emotion" from my heart, and I surrendered it ALL to God.

It was no longer mine to carry and I wasn't about to start packing more emotional baggage into my already over-stuffed luggage of life filled with the hurts of life that I lugged around with me everywhere I went. I was lightening my load by surrendering my ugly, messy "stuff" to God and taking on the yoke of Christ. I wasn't about to fill that puppy back up!

**Matthew 11:29** – *Take My yoke upon you and learn from Me, for I am gentle and lowly in heart, and you will find rest for your souls.* (NKJV)

I went through the boxes of photos and memorabilia and I cried when I needed to, I made scrap books for myself and my children, and stored the rest away in memory boxes to be cherished but kept tucked safely aside out of harm's way, and I prayed A LOT! I mourned what was lost but I made peace with the broken pieces and my past through faith and prayer and by holding on to God through it all.

**Ephesians 4:3** – *Make every effort to keep the unity of the Spirit through the bond of peace.* (NIV)

# Rise and Shine

**Psalm 30:5** – *For His anger is but for a moment, His favor is for life; weeping may endure for a night, but joy comes in the morning.* (NKJV)

The beginning of March brought with it the signs of Spring and new growth. The same was true of me. I felt like I was coming through the fires and feeling renewed. My faith and spirit within me were stronger. I felt more connected to God than ever before and more focused on the things of God: His Word, His people, His direction, His church.

I was fully enlisted in the Army of God and ready to serve in whatever capacity He called me to. I was still hurting and it still wasn't the life I dreamed of, but it was the life I was given and I had a choice to make: to continue to LIVE or not. I chose life by living for God and not myself.

March began with a Women's Night of Worship that was entitled "You Are Enough" at church. It was a wonderful way to begin a new month and to start off a new season in our lives. It was a night of breakthrough for many of the women who attended the service and fellowship.

So many of us were held in bondage to the lies the Enemy has fed us that "I am not _____ enough". We tell ourselves, "I am not good enough, strong enough, pretty enough, smart enough, worthy enough, thin enough…. or simply I am not enough". The lies go on and on. I am sure you can relate; I certainly could.

At the end of the service, Pastor Teresa had a mirror on stage with the words, "I am not _____ enough" written on it. As she finished the service, she shattered the mirror with a hammer; it was a visual illustration of the breaking of chains that was going on in the sanctuary that night. Whatever lie the Enemy has fed you about not being enough, let that lie die now. You were made by the God of more than enough and he made you to ALWAYS be enough!

The first Sunday of March brought with it a visiting pastor who was a friend of our pastors. He gave an amazing sermon with over fifty souls brought to Christ during the two services that morning. His message was titled "When Midnight Comes", and was on **Psalm 119.**

**Psalm 119:62** – *At midnight, I will rise to give thanks to You, because of Your righteous judgements.* (NKJV)

He gave a powerful sermon on what we do at Midnight. I have realized in my journey at Grace, when there is a "Rhema" word (a word that has significance to your soul – like God is speaking it to you directly) for me spoken in a service, it will come up several times during the days before or after. The day before his sermon on Midnight, my daily devotional calendar was on **Exodus 34:2-3** and on the importance of the morning. Several times that week my daily readings were on "rise up" or a variation of it.

**Exodus 34:2-3** – *²So be ready in the morning, and come up in the morning to Mount Sinai, and present yourself to Me there on the top of the mountain. ³And no man shall come up with you, and let no man be seen throughout all the mountain; let neither flocks nor herds feed before that mountain."* (NKJV)

Midnight is the darkest part of the night, the time that the Enemy has the most power. During this season, I had been living the darkest moments of my life: my Midnight. But waiting on the other side of Midnight, there is always dawn breaking through. If you have ever been outside at sun rise, you probably noticed how beautifully painted the sky is to the east; but if you turn to the west, it is still extremely dark with the stars' twinkling as the only ray of light in the darkened sky. It is beautiful really and very peaceful. If you watched it for very long (as I have), you may have noticed how quickly the light from the sun dispels the darkness in the sky. It isn't long before everything is bright and cheerful again.

**Exodus 11:4** – *Then Moses said, "Thus says the Lord: 'About midnight, I will go out into the midst of Egypt;'* (NKJV)

**Acts 27:27** – *Now when the fourteenth had night come, as we were driven up and down in the Adriatic Sea, about midnight the sailors sensed that they were drawing near some land.* (NKJV)

At midnight we are to rise to face the breakthrough that is coming. Even when we don't see it, it is there, hidden in the dark horizon. There are numerous references in the Bible of midnight and what happens after midnight. God struck the first born in Egypt at midnight, Samson went up to the mountain at midnight, Paul and Silas prayed and sang hymns at midnight, Paul preached until midnight, the sailors saw land at midnight, and the bridegroom came at midnight.

**Judges 16:3** – *And Samson lay low till midnight; then he arose at midnight, took hold of the doors of the gate of the city and the two gateposts, pulled them up, bar and all, put them on his shoulders, and carried them to the top of the hill that faces Hebron.* (NKJV)

**Matthew 25:6** – *"And at midnight a cry was heard: 'Behold, the bridegroom is coming; go out to meet him!'* (NKJV)

There are several themes about midnight in the Bible, but the ones I focused on were the following. At midnight, even though it is the darkest moment in our lives and the Enemy's attacks are the strongest, we have to choose to rise up in faith that the storm is breaking around us. At midnight, we are called to praise and pray through the darkness to bring Christ's light to the night as Paul and Silas did (in prison no less). At midnight, we are to focus completely on God, and we are not to get distracted by the fires and storms raging in the darkness surrounding us so that dawn can break through. At midnight, we are to let our old selves, our circumstances, the ties that bind us to our past, the lies the Enemy has told us, and our pasts go and rise up in the full joy of the morning. At midnight, we will break through the darkness with our hand held by God's, guiding us into the light each step of the way.

**Isaiah 41:13** – *For I, the Lord your God, will hold your right hand, saying to you, 'Fear not, I will help you.'* (NKJV)

**Isaiah 9:2** – *The people who walked in darkness have seen a great light; those who dwelt in the land of the shadow of death, upon them a light has shined.* (NKJV)

**Luke 1:78** – *With the loving mercy of our God, a new day from Heaven will dawn upon us.* (NCV)

## PART 2

## SURVIVING THE STORM

### Choose God

**Joshua 24:15** – *And if it seems evil to you to serve the Lord, choose for yourselves this day whom you will serve, whether the gods which your fathers served that were on the other side of the River, or the gods of the Amorites, in whose land you dwell. But as for me and my house, we will serve the Lord.* (NKJV)

The first step to surviving the storms of life is to choose God. Choose God over all your circumstances, over others, over the "things" in your life, and over yourself. Choose God and everything else will fall into place. Choose to give God your heart and all of who you are; and He will give you His grace, His love, His protection, His gifts, and so much more. A life lived by choosing God is so much more fulfilling and beautiful than a life of running from God or pushing Him out of your life.

God loves you and is always there for you. He wants to be a part of your life and to protect you, to guide you, and to take care of you. He wants to walk through the storms of life with you, showing you things from His perspective.

But you must first make the choice of who you will serve and who will be first in your life. It is your choice, but the best way to make it through the storms and fires of life is by choosing God. Who will you choose to serve today?

**Matthew 6:24** – *No one can serve two masters. Either you will hate the one and love the other, or you will be devoted to the one and despise the other. You cannot serve both God and money.* (NIV)

God makes it clear throughout the Bible that we live by freewill, and He desires for us to choose Him freely. Think about the person you love the most in your life. Now imagine that they are bound to you not by love or any desire to truly be with you or to spend time with you, but by obligation or that they are "forced" to spend time with you.

I have tried "forcing" my children to do things together as a family when they were younger and it was never very satisfying, for me or for them. Only if they changed their minds on their own and decided that they wanted to participate and join in the activities freely, were we able to receive any real satisfaction from it. One of my children was very stubborn and obstinate. If he did not want to do something, everyone knew he REALLY didn't want to do it. Forcing him to participate in something he did not want to do only made everyone miserable.

**Psalm 54:6** – *I will freely sacrifice to You, I will praise Your name, O Lord, for it is good.* (NKJV)

In the same way, God does not want us to come to His table kicking and screaming; but of our own free will and with a willing and receptive heart. God wants our love, first and foremost. When you love someone, you desire to spend time with them. How do you show your love to God? You show your love by giving freely of yourself, by CHOOSING to spend time with God, and by putting Him first in your life above all else which is why Jesus said the greatest commandment was to love the Lord with all your heart.

**Matthew 22:37** – *Jesus said to him, "You shall love the Lord your God with all your heart, with all your soul, and with all your mind."* (NKJV)

Life is always about choices and God has given

mankind the freedom to choose who we serve, to choose what we make important in our lives, to choose how we spend our time, and ultimately how we spend eternity. We have the choice to believe or not, to have faith or not, to serve or not.

In my early accounting classes, we studied about opportunity cost and how every choice we make has a cost assigned to it. In its most basic terms, the opportunity cost of any choice we make is the value of the next best option that we are giving up. For example, if I choose to miss work for a day to go to the beach, the opportunity cost of that choice would be the amount of money I would have made had I gone to work. If a father chooses to work late instead of spending time with his family, the opportunity cost is the loss of the value of his time with his family. In the second scenario, the father's choice not only has a cost for him but also for his family as they lost out on the time as well.

I think of the opportunity cost of the choice to not serve God. There is the eternal cost of suffering the fires of Hell and separation from God, but there is also a daily cost. Life is hard but with God there is hope.

Without God, we are living a life in our own strength and capability, which leads us to lead a life of struggle and discontent. The opportunity cost of spending time with God is giving up whatever I might have done instead, such as watching TV or playing on the internet. When I think of all I gain by spending time with God, the opportunity cost of doing so seems minimal while the opportunity cost of not choosing God has eternal ramifications.

**Revelation 3:20** – *Here I am! I stand at the door and knock. If you hear my voice and open the door, I will come in and eat with you, and you will eat with me.* (NKJV)

## Seek God First

How do you Seek God? To seek God first, you must learn who He REALLY is. Most of us have many misconceptions about who God is based on our religious backgrounds, family beliefs, cultural influences, lies fed to us by the Enemy, and other external factors. To truly seek God and keep Him in His proper place at the center of your life and to continually give Him the first-place position in your hearts and lives, you have to learn who He is.

You can do this best by getting into the Word. The Bible is God's gift to us to connect us to Him and who He made us to be. It is a "how to manual" for navigating the storms of life, living for God, seeking eternal life, establishing a relationship with God through Christ and the Holy Spirit, and so much more.

So, who is God?

- God is our Father.
  **2 Corinthians 6:18** – *"I will be a Father to you, and you shall be My sons and daughters, says the Lord Almighty"*. (NKJV)

- God is love!
  **1 John 4:8** – *He who does not love does not know God, for God is love.* (NKJV)

- God is eternal.
  **Psalm 48:14** – *For that is what God is like. He is our God forever and ever, and He will guide us until we die.* (NLT)

- God will teach, instruct and guide you in His ways.
  **Psalm 32:8** – *I will instruct you and teach you in the way you should go; I will guide you with My eye.* (NKJV)

- God will give you the understanding you need.
  **2 Timothy 2:7** – *Consider what I say, and may the Lord give you understanding in all things.* (NKJV)

- God will make you a new creation, with a new heart, and a new mind.
  **2 Corinthians 5:17** – *Therefore, if anyone is in Christ, he is a new creation; old things have passed away; behold, all things have become new.* (NKJV)

- God is faithful.
  **1 Corinthians 1:9** – *God is faithful, by whom you were called into the fellowship of His Son, Jesus Christ our Lord.* (NKJV)

- God is merciful and forgiving.
  **Isaiah 54:9-10** - [9]*"For this is like the waters of Noah to Me; For as I have sworn that the waters of Noah would no longer cover the earth, so have I sworn that I would not be angry with you, nor rebuke you.* [10]*For the mountains shall depart and the hills be removed, but My kindness shall not depart from you, nor shall My covenant of peace be removed," says the Lord, who has mercy on you.* (NKJV)

- God is constant and unchanging.
  **James 1:17** - *Every good gift and every perfect gift is from above, and comes down from the Father of lights, with whom there is no variation or shadow of turning.* (NKJV)

  **Hebrews 13:8** – *Jesus Christ is the same yesterday, today and forever.* (NKJV)

- God is with you ALWAYS!!!
  **Matthew 28:20** – *"Teach these new disciples to obey all the commands I have given you. And be sure of this: I am with you always, even to the end of the age."* (NLT)

- God is your defender and your helper.
  **Hebrews 13:6** – *So we say with confidence, "The Lord is my helper; I will not be afraid. What can man do to me?".* (NIV)

- God is righteous and just.

  **Proverbs 3:11-12 -** *[11]My son, do not despise the Lord's discipline, and do not resent His rebuke, [12]because the Lord disciplines those He loves, as a father the son he delights in.* (NIV)

  **Hebrews 12:5-6** – *[5]And you have forgotten that word of encouragement that addresses you as sons: "My son, do not make light of the Lord's discipline, and do not lose heart when he rebukes you, [6]because the Lord disciplines those He loves, and He punishes everyone He accepts as a son".* (NIV)

  **Hebrews 12:9** – *Since we respected our earthly fathers who disciplined us, shouldn't we submit even more to the discipline of the Father of our spirits, and live forever?* (NLT)

- God can not lie.

  **Numbers 23:19** – *"God is not a man, that He should lie, nor a son of man, that He should repent. Has He said, and will He not do? Or has He spoken, and will He not make it good?"* (NKJV)

- God is our refuge.

  **Deuteronomy 33:27** – *The eternal God is your refuge, and underneath are the everlasting arms; He will thrust out the enemy from before you, and will say, 'Destroy!'* (NKJV)

  **Psalm 62:7** – *In God is my salvation and my glory; the rock of my strength, and my refuge, is in God.* (NKJV)

- God is your strength.
  **2 Samuel 22:33** – *God is my strength and power, and He makes my way perfect.* (NKJV)

- God is for you!
  **Psalm 56:9** – *When I cry out to You, then my enemies will turn back; this I know, because God is for me.* (NKJV)

- God is gracious, merciful and righteous.
  **Psalm 116:5** – *Gracious is the Lord, and righteous; yes, our God is merciful.* (NKJV)

# God, the Father

**1 Corinthians 8:6** – *for us there is only one God – our Father. All things came from Him, and we live for Him. And there is only one Lord – Jesus Christ. All things were made through Him, and we also were made through Him.* (NCV)

**Ephesians 4:6** – *There is one God and Father of everything. He rules everything and is everywhere and is in everything.* (NCV)

As my children got older, I began to think of God as more of a Father; and how He must feel about us the way we feel about our children, but a million times more. We often feel like our children keep pushing us away (especially as they get older and live their own lives); yet we, God's children, often let so many things come before God and push Him out of our lives.

We feel like our children do not appreciate anything we do for them or anything they have; yet God has given us everything we have and ever will have, including the very air we breathe. We still turn away from God and we are not thankful for what He provides.

We feel like our children do not respect us, but we

fail to give God the love, honor and respect He is due. We have let others push God out of our schools, out of our lives, and often even out of Christmas. We feel like our children do not follow our rules and deliberately disobey us, yet how often do we, as God's children, break His commandments and try to hide our sins from Him?

We feel like our children only come to us when they want something, but then we only turn to God when we are truly at our lowest and have nowhere else to turn. Our children never have time for us and in the same way, we often do not make time for God. When we ask our children to do something, they often respond by throwing a fit. When God calls upon us, we respond with "not now", "why me?", or just ignore what He is saying to us. Our children often take us for granted but how much more do we take God for granted?

We know that when we turn away from God and choose the wrong path in life, that He will still always be there waiting, patiently with open arms to welcome us back into His warm embrace. Too often we treat God as a safety net in our lives instead of choosing to make

Him the center of our very existence.

**Malachi 1:6** - *"A son honors his father, and a servant his master. If I am a father, where is the honor due me? If I am a master, where is the respect due me?" says the* LORD *Almighty.* (NIV)

We wonder why we are so off balance and why our children continue to try to find the "easy" way and continue to struggle over and over with the same obstacles we have warned them about. Could it be that they are simply living their lives based on our own actions rather than on our advice? We want to save them the heart ache that we have endured or the dead ends we see them racing towards; yet how often do we pray for them, give them Godly advice, and demonstrate the path of righteousness in our own lives?

I am not saying that all of our children's choices are because of us or are our responsibility; they aren't. Everyone makes their own decisions: right, wrong or otherwise. But our children often have more obstacles to overcome in their lives because they are demonstrating learned behavior from what they have observed their parents doing.

**Romans 8:14** – *For as many as are led by the Spirit of God, these are sons of God.* (NKJV)

When you begin to view God as the loving Father He truly is, it will affect every other area of your life. You will begin to understand His grace and mercy, the compassionate love we are COMMANDED to show one another, and His correction and guidance in our lives when we begin to stray.

**1 John 3:1** – *Behold, what manner of love the Father hath bestowed upon us, that we should be called the sons of God: therefore, the world knoweth us not, because it knew Him not.* (KJV)

**1 John 4:21** – *And this commandment we have from Him: that he who loves God must love his brother also.* (NKJV)

## Get In the Word - Get the Word In You

**Psalm 119:105** – *Your WORD is a lamp to my feet and a light to my path.* (NKJV)

We are all unique individuals and our individual perspectives, our personalities, the way we learn and even the way we connect to God are as unique as we are. Because we are so different, it is important that we each find a Bible version that works for us. My friend enjoys reading the King James Version. I personally find the King James Version more difficult to comprehend, almost like reading a Shakespearean play.

Because I want to truly absorb and understand the Word, I use a bible app that will allow me to look up verses in several versions of the Bible. The New King James Version works well for me, but so does the New Century Version (NCV), New Living Translation (NLT), or the New International Version (NIV).

There are so many different Bible versions and study bibles available, that it is easy to find one that works well for you. The important thing is to find one that you like and that "speaks" to you so that you will be more likely to really get into the Word and get the

Word in you. Find a Bible version that you enjoy reading and will spend time with on a daily basis.

There are numerous translations of the Bible and Bible study tools to use to make understanding and navigating the Word of God easier. I am not going to lecture anyone about their Bible preference or what tools they prefer to use to study the Bible. The important thing is to find a Bible that you enjoy spending time with and can study and really get into. It is the only way to really get to know God and to grow spiritually.

I became a "Devotional Junkie" in my darkest hours. I had a daily bible plan, received numerous emails and daily notifications for daily readings and devotionals, had several devotionals that I read daily, used a daily devotional calendar and used a bible app to follow bible plans and get in the Word each day. I was saturating myself in the Word so there wasn't room for any darkness.

I will admit this was probably a bit overboard, but it worked for me. The point is, you need to find what works for you. There are a lot of great resources available to help you connect with the Word of God. There are podcasts, blogs, online bibles, e-books, hard copy testimonials, bibles, bible studies, and books to choose from.

No matter your taste or preference, there is something out there that will suit you. As long as you are staying connected to God throughout the day and staying in His Word, you are on the right track. One of the challenges for me was how to get to know God and where to start in the Bible.

It can be a bit overwhelming if you don't have a daily reading plan or someone to help guide your way through God's Word. One option that might work for you is a Bible or Devotional that has small scripture readings worked into a daily reading plan.

**2 Timothy 3:16** – *All scripture is given by inspiration of God and is profitable for doctrine, for reproof, for correction, for instruction in righteousness* (NKJV)

If you don't know where to start, you can always begin with the Ten Commandments and be obedient to Christ's teachings and work from there. Proverbs is a great place to start as well. Some people prefer to start with the New Testament and the teachings of Christ. The best advice I can give you is to keep it simple and start out small, so you are not overwhelmed or get burned out.

To make it a part of your daily life, you must be intentional in establishing a routine that works with your schedule, your life and your preferences. You may start out small by reading one scripture a day or one chapter of the Bible a day. You may even ask a friend to read scripture with you daily (together or separately) and then discuss what you each thought of the verses you read. This will help you stay accountable and give you feedback from another person's perspective.

Find what works for you. The most important thing is to continue learning and growing and STAY IN THE WORD because the best way to get to know God is through His Word. When you are focusing on God's Word and dining on a daily diet of biblical scripture, you will begin to see who God is and how you fit into His plan.

**2 Timothy 2:7** – *Consider what I say, and may the Lord give you understanding in all things.* (NKJV)

God will guide you through His Word. He doesn't leave us to wander blindly through life trying to navigate the pitfalls and obstacles on our own. He has always intended to guide us through life through His Word, prayer, His direction, and with the help of the Holy Spirit who dwells within us to guide us. His Word is a manual on how to live our lives God's way.

**Psalm 119:9 –** *How can a young man cleanse his way? By taking heed according to Your word.* (NKJV)

**Proverbs 4:20 –** *My son, give attention to my words; incline your ear to my sayings.* (NKJV)

## Walk in Obedience

**Deuteronomy 13:4** – *You shall walk after the Lord your God and fear Him, and keep His commandments and obey His voice; you shall serve Him and hold fast to Him.* (NKJV)

God tells His children REPEATEDLY to OBEY HIS commands. If you want to know how to make it through the fires and storms of life, the simplest thing (and often the hardest thing) to do is to be obedient to God. To see a breaking in the storms, you must surrender yourself to walk in obedience to the Lord.

**Luke 11:28** – *But He said, "More than that, blessed are those who hear the word of God and keep it!"* (NKJV)

You have to begin to explore His Word because that is where you will find His commands, but God will also guide you through the Holy Spirit within you. He will show you what He wants you to do, but you must be obedient. If you want to know God's Will in your life, you may have to tune everything else out in order to "hear" Him more clearly. I certainly did.

I really struggled with "hearing" God or feeling like I understood the direction He wanted me to go. After months of struggling with this (and lots of Godly guidance from my more seasoned Soul Sisters), I realized I was hearing from God but not in the way I expected.

I expected some sort of instant change when I told God I was "all in" and began living my life fully for Him. Like I would suddenly feel the Holy Ghost within me rising up and KNOW without a shadow of a doubt what God wanted me to do, but that isn't what happened. It took many walks and conversations with God, a great deal of prayer, and self-reflection to realize one of the reasons I didn't suddenly have a Holy Ghost moment was because I had ALWAYS been guided by the Holy Spirit within me.

I was saved as a young teenager (12 or 13 years old), and I had always known Jesus and God. I may not have been seeking God with all my heart or always making Him first in my life, but I have always lived my life as Godly as I could and doing what was right. I had listened to the leadings of the Holy Spirit within me without realizing that was what I was doing most of the time. I was following God even when I wasn't making Him first in my life.

**John 14:15** – *"If you love Me, keep My commandments."* (NKJV)

Even though I didn't "hear" God, I encountered Him frequently in those months when I really needed Him most. God was present in the peace He gave me to help me through the fires and storms. God was also very present in the services, classes, activities, and group meetings I attended at Grace. God would let me know I was on the right path through the "quickening" of the Holy Spirit through my body when I would say certain things. It was as if God was giving me confirmation that what I was speaking was true and lined up with His plan for my life.

There were so many times when I received confirmation through something that was preached in the sermon at church, taught in one of the church classes I took, in one of the devotionals I read, in the conversations I had with other believers, or in one of the Christian books I was reading. God would show me

He was present in my life and was "speaking" to me, even when I did not feel like I was "hearing" anything.

Regardless of how much I desired to "hear" God's guidance in my life and how much I did not feel like I was receiving it, I knew that I had to do my part by being obedient. I had to walk through the storm in obedience and live intentionally for God regardless of how anything looked in the natural. It wasn't easy, and I was still begging God to just let me go; but I wasn't about to do anything to make the situation worse by walking in disobedience to God.

One of the first few classes I took at Grace included a short study on the story of Jonah, and it was a great illustration of what happens when you run from God in disobedience. I wasn't about to even walk in disobedience, much less run from God. I had done that for too many years by not keeping God first in my life and not going to church, by speaking negatively, through allowing my heart to harden with resentment, by holding on to unforgiveness, and many other sins; and it had already cost me too much.

**Deuteronomy 5:33** – *You shall walk in all the ways which the Lord your God has commanded you, that you may live and that it may be well with you, and that you may prolong your days in the land which you shall possess.* (NKJV)

When I surrendered my life fully to God, I recommitted my life to Him and made a covenant with Him to walk in obedience. I might stumble and fall in my walk, but my gracious Heavenly Father would help me get back up and I would plant my feet firmly bank on the path of obedience. The more obedient I was to God, the better I could connect with Him and draw nearer to Him.

**Psalms 1:2** – *But his delight is in the law of the Lord, and in His law he meditates day and night.* (NKJV)

## Soul Sisters and Blood Brothers

**Malachi 2:10** – *Have we not all one father? Has not one God created us? Why do we deal treacherously with one another by profaning the covenant of the fathers?* (NKJV)

**Matthew 12:50** – *For whoever does the will of My Father in heaven is My brother and sister and mother.* (NKJV)

Once you begin a relationship with God, you need to get and stay connected to grow, to not become stagnant, and to be able to withstand the worldly attacks that you will face. Your relationship with God needs to be cultivated so that you can grow nearer to Him and become all He has for you to be. God has limitless blessings that He desires to pour into your life, but you have to continuously seek Him and purposefully stay connected to Him in order to be ready to receive those blessings.

**Mark 3:35** – *"Whoever does God's will is My brother and sister and mother".* (NIV)

God never meant for us to walk through life alone. He is with us always and He has provided avenues in life to help us connect with Him and stay connected. He established "His house" as a place of fellowship, worship, connection, support, guidance, instruction, and so much more. Find a church where you can connect to other believers, receive Godly guidance, and feel closer to God.

**Luke 8:21** – *He replied, "My mother and brothers are those who hear God's word and put it into practice".* (NIV)

To have spiritual growth and to mature in our walk with God, we need to find a place to be fed and a shepherd to guide us. I struggled everywhere I went to find a church that felt like a good fit. Our pastor often said he felt like "a square peg in a round hole" at some of the churches he had attended when he was younger. In some churches, there was no connection to God, the sermons were just lectures. I gravitated more to Sunday school in the churches that had one because at least there I felt like I was being fed.

In my case, I generally went to Southern Baptist churches because I would gravitate to the known. The only part of the service I ever really enjoyed was the singing. I loved the old hymns and that was what we would sing. But when the pastor spoke, it always felt condemning not life affirming.

Don't get me wrong, I believe there has to be a healthy dose of sermons that talk about Hell and the consequences of living an ungodly life. But if that is all you are teaching, you aren't showing anyone how to live a Godly life; just telling them what not to do. It's like telling your child no all the time but never showing them the right choices to make. They will forever feel conflicted and like they are always doing the wrong thing.

I also struggled with feeling connected in church, not just to God but also with fellow church members. There was very little interaction. We would get dressed up in our Sunday best, go to service, and then leave as soon as it was over. I would sit in the back and keep to myself because that is where I was comfortable.

I also felt judged and lacking in church, which made it harder to want to go. Like I said before, church felt like an obligation. I am sure the majority of this feeling was the Enemy's lies that he fed me but I also saw how people in the church treated newcomers, as unwelcome intruders or outsiders. We should embrace new comers. They are seeking the same things we are, and we were once where they are. I always try to welcome any new people in our groups because I remember how awkward and out of place I felt when I first came. It makes me think of the verse where God tells the Israelites to not mistreat a foreigner because you were once a foreigner yourself, yet over and over again throughout the Bible you can see how judgmental, condescending, and hard-hearted the Israelites were especially to those not of their nationality.

**Exodus 22:21** – *"You must not mistreat or oppress foreigners in any way. Remember, you yourselves were foreigners in the land of Egypt."* (NLT)

Pray that God will guide you to the church that is the right "fit" for you. This will probably not mean that you agree with everyone in the congregation or that you will always be touched by God in every service (but it may). It really means that you have to find what works for you. We are all at different spiritual levels and need a different level of teaching. We also all have very different personalities and learn differently, but we need to connect to other believers and find a house of worship where we can worship the Lord in all His awesome glory.

I felt God guiding me to Grace when I came to Killeen and even more so in my moments of broken-ness. But even then, I looked up various churches on line and watched their online service. I read the Mission Statements and the values of each church. I prayed that God would lead me where I needed to go, and He did.

Trust the Holy Spirit to be your guide. If something in a church doesn't feel right in your Spirit, then it may not be the best fit for you. Be open to the leading of the Spirit and "lean not on your own understanding". Remember the Enemy will also try to drive you away from church because He does not want you to connect with or grow in your relationship with God.

I used to think you didn't have to go to church to be a Christian; and while this is technically true, it leaves you a lot more lonely and vulnerable to the attacks of the Enemy than when you are walking arm in arm with other believers. Get into church. Don't find excuses not to go. God wants to meet you there. Make a commitment to honor Him with your time and meet Him in His house with your Soul Sisters and Blood Brothers in Christ.

**Romans 8:29** – *For God knew His people in advance, and He chose them to become like His Son, so that His Son would be the firstborn among many brothers and sisters.* (NLT)

There is power in numbers. We are ALL children of God (regardless of our sex, nationality, color, ethnicity, beliefs or anything else). Once you accept Christ into your heart, and you are filled with the Holy Spirit; you become bonded even closer to other believers through your faith, your love of God, the covering of the Blood of Christ, and the renewal of your heart and soul in the Holy Spirit. We are all soldiers in God's Army called to spread His love and light, and the knowledge of Him to our fallen brothers and sisters. A unified voice rises higher than the individual voices of many. Add your single voice to the multitude of God's children in calling for the lost.

**Matthew 18:20** – *For where two or three are gathered together in My name, there I am in the midst of them.* (KJV)

## Seek Godly Wisdom

**Colossians 1:9-12** – *[9]For this reason we also, since the day we heard it, do not cease to pray for you, and to ask that you may be filled with the knowledge of His will in all wisdom and spiritual understanding; [10]that you may walk worthy of the Lord, fully pleasing Him, being fruitful in every good work and increasing in the knowledge of God; [11]strengthened with all might, according to His glorious power, for all patience and longsuffering with joy; [12]giving thanks to the Father who has qualified us to be partakers of the inheritance of the saints in the light.* (NKJV)

The second recommendation I would make to grow closer to God is to find a spiritual mentor. A few weeks into my journey at Grace, I became fast friends with a woman in our Thursday Night Women's study who was an Evangelist and would intercede in prayer for the women in the group. I met Erica on my second night at Grace, and I was struck with her presence and knowledge of the Word. She knew the Bible very well and could quote scripture and verse on nearly any subject in the Bible.

By stepping out of my comfort zone and approaching her to intercede for my husband in prayer,

I opened the door to a close friendship that became mutually beneficial to us both. We are almost complete opposites in personality, but sometimes that is a good thing. That night, when I approached her after class, Erica invited me to her house for fellowship, and I didn't leave until almost midnight. Through our hours together, my story tumbled out in a mixture of broken sobs and babble. But it was enough for Erica to see the heart of the issue, and she offered to mentor me. I remember asking her "where do I start?".

You may have found yourself asking this same question. I had no idea how to "find" God although I was seeking Him with everything in me. It didn't seem to matter how hard I tried, I just didn't feel like I could hear God. The issue was that God wasn't lost, I was. I needed help finding MY WAY, learning how to connect with God, and recognizing when He was speaking to me.

Erica loaned me a daily Devotional and a work book on getting to know Jesus (when seeking the Father, it really helps to know the Son first). Having a spiritual mentor or guide really makes a difference when you are lost. They can help you find your way back to where you need to be and help you reconnect to God.

This person does not have to be a Pastor, Evangelist or other titled person within the church; they just need to be a Godly person who can help guide you through Godly wisdom. Pray that God will send the person across your path that will help you to know Him better and to guide your way through the challenges of gaining Godly wisdom. I was fortunate to have several such Godly women in my life at that time, including Mrs. Jackie, Erica, Catherine, and Keneshia (the other friends I made in my early days at Grace).

**Proverbs 4:6** – *Do not forsake wisdom, and she will protect you; love her, and she will watch over you.* (NIV)

Speaking of the friends I made in our Women's Group, my next recommendation is for you to join a support group. Whether you begin counselling, join a fellowship group, a Bible study, or join a non-Christian support group: seek out others who can understand what you are going through and can offer support, advice, and comfort when you need it most.

So many of us are used to carrying our burdens and pain alone, that we withdraw from the outside world and isolate ourselves. I am not saying broadcast your pain and circumstances to everyone you meet, but find someone you can talk to. Withdrawing inside yourself without finding a Godly outlet can be very self-destructive.

In my case, I started going to counselling to deal with my repressed issues and to have a safe, non-judgmental, and confidential place to discuss my pain and circumstances. I also joined Mrs. Jackie's Women's Bible Study. Joining the Women's Bible Study was the best decision I made. It became an anchor I could hold on to when I was in my darkest moments. It also gave me Godly connections to call on when I really needed prayer the most to face the fires and storms raging in my life.

**Proverbs 4:7** – *Wisdom is the most important thing; so get wisdom. If it costs everything you have, get understanding.* (NCV)

Whatever you do, DO NOT ISOLATE yourself

completely. This is a very self-destructive behavior and will cause more damage in your already broken circumstances. It is easy to do this when you are in pain. Hurting people often want to go hide in a cave somewhere and lick their wounds and heal in private.

You may need some time alone to grieve and to heal but this should not be an all day, every day affair. If you disconnect from the world completely, it will be more difficult to adjust to the outside world when you decide to. It also leaves you alone and more vulnerable to the attacks and lies of the Enemy.

We often need the love and support of one another and this is even more true when you are hurting. To know that someone else has been through the storm that you are now facing and came out the other side victorious, with God by their side provides true hope that you can survive.

As Christians, we are survivors, overcomers, victors (not victims); and YOU ARE NOT ALONE. No matter what your walk may be, no matter what your circumstances, no matter what you may or may not have done in your past: someone else has been where you are. If we just continue sharing our stories with one another and encouraging one another; we will realize that other people do understand, they have been there and we are not alone.

**1 John 4:4** – *You are of God, little children, and have overcome them, because He who is in you is greater than he who is in the world.* (NKJV).

It is important that we help our brothers and sisters in Christ to know they have a support system behind them and they are not alone. This is just as true for men as it is for women. We are often our own worst critic, but we need to set aside our pride and call on our brothers or sisters in Christ to help us find our way through the storm. We can do more together than we ever possibly could on our own.

**Ecclesiastes 4:12** – *Though one may be overpowered by another, two can withstand him. And a threefold cord is not quickly broken.* (NKJV)

## P.U.S.H. Through the Storm

**Jeremiah 33:3** – *"Call to me and I will answer you, and show you great and mighty things, which you do not know."* (NKJV)

I have heard many people say "P.U.S.H" your way through your trials and tribulations, short for "Pray Until Something Happens". I agree with this saying and that there is great power in prayer; however, I think there is a second part to this. I believe you not only have to "Pray Until Something Happens", but you also have to "Praise Until Something Happens".

**1 Thessalonians 5:17** – *Pray without ceasing.* (KJV)

I believe we also have to be cognizant that the "something" may not be the thing we WANT or are waiting for. It is going to be God's answer, whether that is 'Yes', 'No', 'Wait', etc. That "something" can just as likely be a change in our hearts or in our desires as it is receiving the answer to our prayers that we were seeking. Remember that God knows the big picture and knows what is right and just. In our limited sight, we only see our little section of the giant jigsaw puzzle of life. From God's perspective, He sees the completed picture that the puzzle will be, not just the broken fragments that we see.

**Psalm 7:17** – *I will praise the Lord according to His righteousness, and will sing praise to the name of the Lord Most High.* (NKJV)

**Psalm 69:30** – *I will praise the name of God with a song, and will magnify Him with thanksgiving.* (NKJV)

In the immortal words of Dory, "Just keep swimming". It doesn't matter how big your storm is, your God is bigger and mightier. Sometimes He will calm the storms around you and sometimes He will guide you safely through the storms. Just keep praying and holding on to God as your lifeline. He will always get you through. He is unsinkable!

**Psalm 89:9** – *You rule the raging of the sea; when its waves rise, You still them.* (NKJV).

**Isaiah 25:4** – *For you have been a strength to the poor, a strength to the needy in his distress, a refuge from the storm, a shade from the heat; for the blast of the terrible ones is as a storm against the wall.* (NKJV)

But we must do our part to weather the storms as well. We must believe and pray and not give up. I know it is not that easy; but honey, no one ever said life was easy and if they did, they were lying. Christ even said we will have troubles in this life (**John 16:33**). Life is hard and sometimes it plain ol' sucks. But God is always there, with His hand in yours, guiding you through the storms and fires of life. You are never alone nor are you required to do it in your own strength!

**Psalm 145:18-19 -** *[18]The Lord is near to all who call upon Him, to all who call upon Him in truth. [19]He will fulfill the desire of those who fear Him; He also will hear their cry and saves them. (NKJV)*

If you fall, that's okay too. Just as soon as you can catch your breath, get back on your feet and take the next step, and then another and another, and keep going forward. Life will go on with us or without us. No matter how much it hurts, life will always go on. It is much better for you if you can move forward, even if it is only one inch at a time. Keep your focus on God and keep moving forward.

**Psalm 54:2 –** *Listen to my prayer, O God. Pay attention to my plea.* (NLT)

If you are like me and aren't sure how to really "praise" God, the book of Psalms is a great place to start. King David (the author of the book of Psalms) knew a thing or two about Praise and Worship. He also had a lot of repenting to do. He was definitely one of the broken people of the Bible that God used for His glory and honor. He praises the Lord throughout the Psalms, regardless of the tribulations he was facing in life. Look up scripture on praising God. The Lord loves hearing His Word on our lips as we worship and honor Him.

Another great way to learn how to praise God is to listen to Praise and Worship music. Whether you prefer the old school hymns, the hip-hop Christian music artists or the Contemporary Christian artists; there is plenty of good Godly worship music to choose from. Begin to really listen to the words and open your heart to the Lord as you sing them out. You don't have to be a great singer, I certainly am not. Our voices are beautiful to God. He made them after all.

**Psalm 68:4** – *Sing to God; sing praises to His name. Prepare the way for Him who rides through the desert, whose name is the Lord. Rejoice before Him.* (NCV)

We are all unique and we all have different likes and dislikes. I for one, didn't really care for the

Contemporary Christian Music, preferring the old hymns that I grew up with. However, when I was the most broken, there were several songs that spoke to my heart and soul, and gave me comfort in my greatest time of need. I won't mention them here, but there were several that I would play over and over in my darkest moments and they helped pull me through.

Sometimes I would just sing the songs I learned in children's church like "Jesus Loves Me This I Know" and "He's Got the Whole World in His Hands". It doesn't matter what you sing or how you praise, it is the condition of your heart that matters. Whatever makes you feel closer to God, do that. Ask other Christians what they listen to or search Christian songs or radio stations, if you don't know any. The most important thing is to find a way to praise God that works for you and that you will stick with.

**Hebrews 13:15** – *Therefore by Him let us continually offer the sacrifice of praise to God, that is the fruit of our lips, giving thanks to His name.* (NKJV)

The next piece of advice I have on seeking and praising God is to be thankful. Don't just be thankful when life is good, but be thankful in ALL things, even the hurtful ones. Be thankful for the things you don't see, for God's goodness through it all, for not having to endure it alone, for God making a way for you to make it through. This is often even harder than it sounds. We forget to be thankful to God for the multitude of good things in our lives and now we have to be thankful for the bad ones too?

**Psalm 100:1-4 –** [1]*Make a joyful noise unto the Lord, all ye lands.* [2]*Serve the Lord with gladness: come before His presence with singing.* [3]*Know ye that the Lord He is God: it is He that hath made us, and not we ourselves; we are His people, and the sheep of His pasture.* [4]*Enter into His gates with thanksgiving, and into His courts with praise: be thankful unto Him, and bless His name.* (KJV)

There is so much more to it than that: being thankful not only glorifies the Father but it changes the condition of your heart. It becomes a part of who you are and it becomes so much easier to be thankful in all things when you stop focusing on the negatives and just thank God for them. It helps us to let them go. It also shows God where our hearts really are and just how much He really means to us.

God is the master at turning our circumstances

around; but sometimes He may want you to be thankful that you are in the situation in the first place so that His glory can shine through. Troubles build your faith and your reliance and trust in God. Be thankful that they draw you nearer to Him if nothing else. The best thing to do is to thank God for being with you through the bad times, and ask Him what you can learn from it. If you have to go through it anyway, there might as well be some benefit to it.

One of the things I learned to be thankful for was the things God was blocking that I wasn't even aware of. We all know that God fights our battles for us, but have you ever stopped to think about the attacks that came and He shielded you from them so completely that you weren't even aware of them?

**Deuteronomy 20:4** – *For the Lord your God is going with you! He will fight for you against your enemies, and He will give you victory!* (NLT)

One day the devotional I was reading talked about thanking God for the things He blocked in your life. I had never really thought about that. I thanked God daily for all He has gifted me with (including my children and the very breath in my lungs), for the troubles that I face, and for who He is; but I had never thought about thanking Him for the things He blocked from ever even reaching me. As soon as I spoke the prayer, I had such a quickening in my spirit and I knew that God had blocked some powerful things from even my awareness, much less my life.

One night shortly before this, my friend was praying with me in her car and she told me the Devil was trying to take my life. I hadn't felt the attacks or had any further suicidal thoughts in several weeks. I felt more at peace about it, but I couldn't dismiss what she said. She is a Godly woman and I knew she spoke the truth; but I didn't feel like I was under attack.

There were times I knew the Enemy was attacking me directly. I remember lying in bed one night, praying (and crying) to the Lord about my marriage, my husband, and my brokenness; and I suddenly heard, very clearly, another voice in my thoughts saying, "It's too late. You have been defeated. I have already won.".

It was a very heavy man's voice and it sent chills through my body. I immediately rebuked it and spoke out loud in faith that God would work out all things for my good, and that the Devil was a liar and could go back to the pit of Hell where he crawled out of. But I would be lying if I said it didn't seriously rock me. It filled me with such despair and foreboding when I first heard that voice. It was like icy fingers running down my spine.

I had felt the attacks very clearly at times, such as during my thoughts of taking the gun; but it suddenly became very clear that there were so many more attacks that I wasn't even aware of, that God had completely blocked from even reaching my consciousness. I feel like I can say with confidence the same is probably true for you as well. Take a minute and thank God for all that He has blocked from reaching you and all that He has protected you from that you have never even been aware of.

**1 Thessalonians 5:18** – *in everything give thanks; for this is the will of God in Christ Jesus for you.* (NKJV)

# Live Like Christ

**Isaiah 9:6** – *For unto us a Child is born, unto us a Son is given; and the government will be upon His shoulder. And His name will be called Wonderful, Counselor, Mighty God, Everlasting Father, Prince of Peace.* (NKJV)

**Philippians 2:5** – *In your lives, you must think and act like Christ Jesus.* (NCV)

Life is about choices and if you want to survive the fires and storms of life; you will often have to make some difficult and uncomfortable ones. We are called throughout the Bible to live a Christ-like life. This will often mean doing things we don't really want to do in our flesh.

If you look at the attributes of Christ; He was loving regardless of the person or circumstance, accepting not condemning, peaceful and joyful. He loved the unlovable, healed the broken, befriended the discarded, sought out the lost, responded in love, encouraged all to seek God's Kingdom, and gave hope and faith to those in despair. It is not possible on our own to live such a life; but with God, all things are possible. God will help us to live such a life (in our own walk and with our own Spiritual Gifts from above) through the love of Christ and the guidance of the Holy Spirit within us.

**Matthew 19:26** – *But Jesus looked at them and said to them, "With men this is impossible, but with God all things are possible."* (NKJV)

To live more Christlike, you will have to learn who Christ is. There are so many names of Christ in scripture, but I will include a small list here.

Christ is: the Son of God, our Savior, the Prince of Peace, the Messiah, the Lamb of God, our Counselor, the good shepherd, our Redeemer, the Lion of Judah, our mediator, the Rock, the way to God, Prince of Life, the Resurrection and Life, wholly innocent and blameless, without sin, the Truth, the Light, the Way, and the Word. He is so much more than can be stated in these few words and there is a great deal of scripture to help you find for yourself who Christ is. I encourage you to find the truth about Christ in God's Word for yourself.

To live a more Christlike life, we need to look at His character. Christ was loving, forgiving, patient, kind, joyful, life giving, full of peace, truthful, encouraging, compassionate, wise, self-sacrificing, tolerant, humble, fearless and brave. Christ lived to serve and sacrificed His very life for each and every one of us: for you, for me; for the lost and the found; for the sinners and the saints. He is not judgmental or harsh.

He showed compassionate kindness wherever He went. He was gentle, loving, patient, and kind. He was fruitful and full of the fruit of the Holy Spirit. He was obedient to the point of laying down His very life so we could all be saved and have a relationship with the Father as well as with Christ. He loves us so much that He faced brutality, scorn and ridicule, doubt, hatred, anger, condemnation, disbelief, torture, mockery, and a horrific and painful death so that we may LIVE forever and be saved.

He is all of these things still and so much more. His gift does not expire and will never be taken away; it was and is freely given. He said it Himself that He does not give to us as the world gives. Trust me when I say there is no exchange or return policy with God on His gifts. I've been looking to return my life for a while but

He continues to say no. Seek Christ and ask Him to help you see who He really is and how much you mean to Him.

**John 14:27** – *"I leave you peace; my peace I give you. I do not give it to you as the world does. So don't let your hearts be troubled or afraid.* (NCV)

We often return Christ's most awesome gift with selfishness, greed, spite, pride, rejection, anger, resentment, defiance, etc. Make the decision to value the gift He has given you and return that gift with love and obedience. Follow His example in how to live your life by fostering growth of the Fruit of the Holy Spirit in your life, and you will find true happiness and joy.

There will be pain and sorrows (there are pain and sorrows in life anyway); but in Christ, we have a defender and a helper to make it through the painful fires and storms we face in this life. We have hope in the life after this. Choose life.

Give freely to others, put their needs before your own; forgive those who have hurt you and pray for them rather than seeking revenge against them; show compassion and mercy to others rather than condemning or judging them; treat everyone with loving kindness, even when you really don't feel like it. Develop the fruit of the Spirit in your own character. Learn to control your emotions and your mouth. This may require more prayer too.

Pray daily that God will give you a heart like Jesus. Set aside your pride and your own wants and desires and ask God to show you His desires for your life. Humble yourself before the Lord and seek His favor first and foremost in your life. You may be amazed at how fulfilling a Christ-like life can be.

**Galatians 5:22-23** – *[22]But the fruit of the Spirit is love, joy, peace, patience, kindness, goodness, faithfulness, [23]gentleness and self-control. Against such things there is no law.* (NIV)

## Stay in Your Lane

**John 14:26** – *But the Helper, the Holy Spirit, whom the Father will send in My name, He will teach you all things, and bring to your remembrance all things that I have said to you.* (NKJV)

I am a terrible bowler. No matter how well I aim for the middle of the pins or how straight my shot seems at the beginning; it always ends up in the gutter, veering off to the right or to the left. Because I can't bowl worth a darn, I use bumpers. You know, those pads they put up to block the gutters for little kids? Yeah, those.

That is how I often imagined my travels through life with the Holy Spirit as my guide. He is directing me straight down the middle of the lane, with God at the center as my focus. The lane may be wider or narrower in some areas but He has bumpers at the edge to help keep me in my lane. When I hit the bumper, it gently guides me back to the middle. That doesn't mean that I cannot leave my lane, but it does mean that I have to be really out of control or I have to be intentionally trying to go beyond the bumper zone to leave my lane.

**Deuteronomy 5:32** – *Therefore you shall be careful to do as the Lord your God has commanded you; you shall not turn aside to the right hand or to the left.* (NKJV)

We can still swing wildly and end up two lanes over if we are trying to do it all in our own strength or in our own way, ignoring the Holy Spirit's guiding; but the more we adhere to His whispered guidance, the straighter our path will be. Trust the Holy Spirit within you to be your guide.

**Isaiah 45:2** – *"I will go before you and make the crooked places straight; I will break in pieces the gates of bronze and cut the bars of iron".* (NKJV)

**Psalm 143:10** – *Teach me to do Your will, for You are my God; may Your good Spirit lead me on level ground.* (NIV)

**2 Thessalonians 3:5** – *Now may the Lord direct your hearts into the love of God and into the patience of Christ.* (NKJV)

**Psalm 25:9** – *The humble He guides in justice, and the humble He teaches His way.* (NKJV)

The same way the Ark of the Covenant went before the people of Israel so that they would know which way to go as they had never been there before, trust that the Holy Spirit will lead you through the unknown journeys in your life. God doesn't leave us to wander blindly through our lives but gives us a guide to help us through the journey and to tell us when we are taking a wrong turn.

There are times our path seems more like the yellow brick road with many bricks missing, winding through dark forests, poisonous flowers, and endless fields; but if you trust the wisdom of the Holy Spirit to help you through those gaps in the road, to provide the light you need through the darkness, and to guide you on the direction you should go; you can lighten your load and leave worry, fear, and anxiety behind, knowing you will make it safely to the end.

**Joshua 3:4** – *"That way you will know which way to go since you have never been here before. But do not follow too closely. Stay about a thousand yards behind the Ark."* (NCV)

**2 Corinthians 13:14** – *The grace of the Lord Jesus Christ, and the love of God, and the communion of the Holy Spirit be with you all. Amen.* (NKJV)

It may be difficult for you to understand who the Holy Spirit is or to comprehend His role in your life. I struggled with fully grasping the concept of the Holy

Spirit because I was thinking logically instead of spiritually. It helped me to learn more about Him and who He is as well as His place in my life. By getting to know Him better through the Word and by daily communion with Him, I began to better understand who He is and His character. He is my constant companion and I am grateful that He is always with me, guiding my way.

**Isaiah 30:21** – *Your ears shall hear a word behind you, saying, "This is the way, walk in it," whenever you turn to the right hand or whenever you turn to the left.* (NKJV)

I always pictured Him as my inner compass, guiding me through life, letting me know when I was getting off the path I was to take. As I grew closer to God and matured in my Christian faith and walk, I also was more aware of the Holy Spirit's presence in my daily life. I was more attuned to Him and His guidance.

I believe He is more often than not misunderstood and disregarded by so many of us. But if we allow Him in our hearts and heed His guidance in our lives, He will show us the way and teach us all we need to know. I encourage you to get to know Him better. Talk to

Him, ask Him to show you the things He wants to show you, spend time with Him. I talk to the Holy Spirit in my prayers (or out loud when I need to work through something), the same as I talk to God and Christ.

Here is what I have learned about the Holy Spirit. The Holy Spirit will teach you the things of God, He will bring them to your remembrance, He will give you the understanding and revelation that you need, and He will guide you on your path in this life. He is a gift to those who believe; He is within you; He is the Helper; He speaks through you; He gives you the Spiritual Gifts; He will teach you and guide you; He comforts you; He empowers you; He will bring you peace, hope, love, joy, and self-control; He is our Counselor; He is with you ALWAYS; He is your Intercessor and unites you with God and with each other. I encourage you right now to ask the Holy Spirit to show you who He is and how you can get to know Him better.

**John 14:16-17** – *[16]And I will pray the Father, and He will give you another Helper, that He may abide with you forever— [17]the Spirit of truth, whom the world cannot receive, because it neither sees Him nor knows Him; but you know Him, for He dwells with you and will be in you.* (NKJV)

**John 14:18** – *I will not leave you orphans; I will come to you.* (NKJV)

**Luke 12:12** – *For the Holy Spirit will teach you in that very hour what you ought to say.* (NKJV)

**Luke 11:13** – *If you then, being evil, know how to give good gifts to your children, how much more will your heavenly Father give the Holy Spirit to those who ask Him!"* (NKJV)

Another way to get to know the Holy Spirit better and to learn more about yourself is to take a Spiritual Gifts assessment. Once you take the assessment, research what each of your gifts are: their strengths, their weaknesses, what the Bible says about each gift. Your Spiritual Gifts are a huge part of who you are as a person. It really is in your best interest to learn more about them so you can develop them to be used as God meant for you to use them and so you can keep the Enemy from using them against you. Trust me, he will every chance he has.

**1 Corinthians 12:4** – *There are different kinds of gifts, but they are all from the same Spirit.* (NCV)

# Conviction Not Confliction

**1 Corinthians 14:33** – *For God is not the author of confusion, but of peace, as in all churches of the saints.* (KJV)

**Romans 8:1** – *There is therefore now no condemnation to those who are in Christ Jesus, who do not walk according to the flesh, but according to the Spirit.* (NKJV)

So often in our lives, the Enemy will use our lack of knowledge and understanding against us. He knows that he can use our limited understanding of God and His ways to twist our thinking to make us feel guilty and condemned about our wrongdoings. God loves us regardless of our sins. He loves us ALWAYS, there is no end to His love or to the lengths He will go for us. There is no condemnation in God.

God, through the Holy Spirit, will convict us of our wrongdoings and then guide us to the right path. He knows our weaknesses and our failures, but He loves us anyway and always provides a way to bring us back in line with Him. Webster defines conviction the best as, "the act of convincing a person of error or of compelling the admission of truth". Webster also defines condemnation as a declaration of guilt or reprehensible wrongdoing, or of evil. One of the greatest weapons the Enemy likes to use against us is our own insecurities and lack of self-worth; our sense of guilt, shame and condemnation.

If you are feeling conflicted, confused or condemned; this is NOT from God. When we sin, it grieves God, and He will let us know that we have grieved Him. You will feel His conviction through the Holy Spirit, but His conviction is not like that of the world and it is not condemning. God's ways are higher than anything we could possibly imagine. When we sin, He will show us the truth and offer us a chance to repent but with His grace and not by condemnation.

He will not beat us over the head with our sins and transgressions or make us suffer undue guilt over anything we have done. He will urge us to do what is right and just and gently guide us in His ways so we can repent and when possible, make amends for our ways.

The Enemy likes to manipulate our thoughts and self-doubts to make us feel less than, unworthy, dirty, shameful, guilty, unforgiven; but he is a Master

Manipulator and the King of Liars. Do not buy into the lies he is trying to sell you and do not let him steal your peace or joy with his lies. When you are feeling conflicted or condemned, stop and ask God to show you the truth and His thoughts towards you. God's truth is our best weapon against the lies of the Enemy.

**Isaiah 55:8-9** – *[8]"For my thoughts are not your thoughts, nor are your ways My ways," says the Lord. [9]"For as the heavens are higher than the earth, so are My ways higher than your ways, and My thoughts than your thoughts."* (NKJV)

**Psalm 32:5** – *I acknowledged my sin to You, and my iniquity I have not hidden. I said, "I will confess my transgressions to the Lord,". And You forgave the iniquity of my sin. Selah* (NKJV)

**1 Corinthians 10:13** – *The temptations in your life are no different from what others experience. And God is faithful. He will not allow the temptation to be more than you can stand. When you are tempted, He will show you a way out so that you can endure.* (NLT)

## Focus on the Light

**Isaiah 60:20** – *Your sun will never set again, and your moon will never be dark, because the Lord will be your light forever, and your time of sadness will end.* (NCV)

**Psalm 123:2** – *Behold, as the eyes of servants look to the hand of their masters, as the eyes of a maid to the hand of her mistress, so our eyes look to the Lord our God, until He has mercy on us.* (NKJV)

God wants to be the focus of your life, not just because He desires to be at the center of your life but because he knows that is what is best for you. When we focus completely on God and keep Him as the center of our lives, we are able to accomplish all that He has called us to do.

When a child first begins to walk, he will often be able to stand or even take a few steps as he stays focused on his mother, encouraging him forward with "come to momma". But as soon as he takes his eyes off his mother and realizes that no one is holding him up, he will lose balance and fall. Why? Because as long as his gaze is on his mother's loving face, he has the confidence he needs to stand on his own. Once he drops his gaze, he loses that connection that gives him the courage and faith to do what was otherwise impossible for him to do.

The same is true for us. As long as we keep our eyes focused on God, we are able to walk through the fires of life with little thought to our surroundings. But as soon as we take our gaze off God, we will begin to stumble and fall. We allow doubt and fear to convince us that we cannot do what God has already equipped us to do. When God is our focus, we are able to walk in faith without being distracted by the storms raging in our lives, guided in His path by the Holy Spirit within us, walking in His perfect peace.

**Isaiah 26:3 –** *You will keep him in perfect peace, whose mind is stayed on You, because he trusts in You.* (NKJV)

Think about Peter walking on the water as long as he focused his gaze on Jesus; but once he looked down at the water, he began to sink. He shifted his gaze from Christ to his circumstances and realized he was doing something that was beyond him. But that is the wondrous thing; when we focus on God, we are able to do what would otherwise be impossible on our own because we are doing it through His strength and not our own.

God wants us to focus on Him because He knows that He will get us through any challenges we may face. We stumble when we lose faith and remove our gaze from Him. God doesn't want us to get distracted by the waves of life but to keep Him as our focus so we can walk through the parted sea and make it safely to the other side. Believe that He is there with you walking through the parted waters and protecting you from the destruction of the Evil One.

**Jeremiah 29:13** – *And you will seek Me and find Me, when you search for Me with all your heart.* (NKJV)

**Psalm 139:7** – *Where can I go from Your Spirit? Or where can I flee from Your presence?* (NKJV)

God is there....when you can't feel it, when you can't see Him, when you can't hear Him, when it feels like you can never connect to Him....God is there with you cradled in His hands. Trust that He will never leave you nor forsake you. Even better, stand confidently in the knowledge that nothing can ever separate you from the love of God. Why is that? Because God IS love and there is nothing in the world greater than God! Even when you feel completely alone in the world, stand on God's promises in His word that He will ALWAYS be with you.

**Hebrews 13:5** – *Keep your lives free from the love of money and be content with what you have, for God has said, "Never will I leave you; never will I forsake you".* (NIV)

**Romans 8:37-39** – *[37]Yet in all these we are more than conquerors through Him who loved us. [38]For I am persuaded that neither death nor life, nor angels nor principalities nor powers, nor things present nor things to come, [39]nor height, nor depth, nor any other created thing, shall be able to separate us from the love of God which is in Christ Jesus our Lord.* (NKJV)

So why do I say that we should focus on the light? Because God is the source of light and wants to be our guiding light in all circumstances. Throughout scripture, we are told the light will lead the way and guide us, the light will shine on us, that we are to be a light in the world to draw others to God, the light drives out the darkness, light brings knowledge, and light shows what is hidden and exposes sin. God shines His light on us. When we focus on the light, we begin to draw nearer to the light. Throughout scripture, we are told of the guiding lights God used to show people the way: the wise men followed the light of the star, the Israelites followed the light by night out of Egypt, and Christ himself was the light in the world drawing those in the world to Him. We are even told that our feet are guided by the light or lamp to show us the path we are to walk in this life.

**John 8:12** – *Then Jesus spoke to them again, saying, "I am the light of the world. He who follows Me shall not walk in darkness, but have the light of life."* (NKJV)

Did you know that sunflowers will always follow the light? It's kind of amazing to watch and you can look up videos showing the time lapse where the sunflowers turn their "faces" throughout the day to follow the sun's path in the sky. If you know anything about plants, you know that they need light to grow. The sunflower has an innate ability to seek the life sustaining power of the light. The plants will begin the day facing the east and the sunrise and will reposition themselves throughout the day to get the most sun. It looks like they are turning their "faces" to face the light at all times. I believe we are to live our lives like the sunflower and turn our faces continuously to the light of our Heavenly Father.

**1 John 1:7** – *But if we walk in the light as He is in the light, we have fellowship with one another, and the blood of Jesus Christ His Son cleanses us from all sin.* (NKJV)

**Isaiah 42:6** – *The Lord says, "I, the Lord, called you to do right, and I will hold your hand and protect you. You will be the sign of my agreement with the people, a light to shine for all people."* (NCV)

**Numbers 6:25** – *The Lord make His face shine upon you, and be gracious to you.* (NKJV)

# Walk by Faith

**1 Corinthians 13:13** – *Three things will last forever – faith, hope, and love – and the greatest of these is love.* (NLT)

**Faith:**

**2 Corinthians 5:7** – *For we walk by faith, not by sight.* (NKJV)

**Mark 11:22** – *So Jesus answered and said to them, "Have faith in God."* (NKJV)

**1 Corinthians 2:5** – *that your faith should not be in the wisdom of men but in the power of God.* (NKJV)

**Luke 8:48** – *And He said to her, "Daughter, be of good cheer; your faith has made you well. Go in peace."* (NKJV)

Keep moving forward in faith. Webster defines faith as, "firm belief in something for which there is no proof; complete trust". Faith is believing without seeing. It is knowing that God is there without ever seeing Him face to face. Faith is eternal and once you plant the seed of faith in your life, it will grow beyond measure. Faith is knowing that no matter how dark your circumstances may be, God is the light at the end of the tunnel rather than a train headed straight for you, like it often may seem. Faith is holding on to God as your rock in the storms of life and knowing that He has you in His hands.

Faith is Noah building an ark without rain. Faith is Moses confronting Pharaoh with nothing but a staff. Faith is parting the Red Sea by believing he can. Faith is knowing that I am God's beloved daughter, and He wants only the best for me even when it seems like only the worst is happening in my life. Faith is believing there is a better beginning after the end of this life. Faith isn't always easy or comfortable but it will get you through when you have nothing left. Faith is praying for your lost loved ones even when there seems to be no hope.

Let your faith ignite a small spark in your heart and as it is fed, it will become a raging fire. Faith heals, faith opens doors, faith moves, faith saves, faith provides, faith fights, faith believes, faith overcomes, and faith ignites hope.

**Hebrews 11:1** – *Now faith is the substance of things hoped for, the evidence of things not seen.* (NKJV)

**Hope:**

**Matthew 17:20** – *He replied, "Because you have so little faith. I tell you the truth, if you have faith as small as a mustard seed, you can say to this mountain, 'Move from here to there,' and it will move. Nothing will be impossible for you."* (NIV)

**Romans 5:2** – *through whom we have gained access by faith into this grace in which we now stand. And we boast in the hope of the glory of God.* (NIV)

**Galatians 5:5** – *For we through the Spirit eagerly wait for the hope of righteousness by faith.* (NKJV)

Through faith hope is born. Webster defines hope as "to cherish a desire with anticipation", "to desire with expectation of obtainment or fulfillment", and "to expect with confidence". As Christians, we often allow the Enemy to kill our hope, steal our joy, and destroy our faith. To combat this, we have to fuel our hope through faith.

Reading the definitions above reminds me of how our hope is in the Lord, not of things of this world. Because we live in the world and have experienced great disappointments, being let down by those we love, having our faith in others betrayed; we struggle with our faith in the Lord. To have true faith (and remember the smallest amount of faith can move mountains), we have to stop thinking with our worldly mind and believe with our renewed mind of Christ.

God will NEVER fail you or let you down. He may not do exactly what you want but that's probably because what you want is fleeting or isn't good for you, but God is ALWAYS faithful. Invest your faith in God and you will receive an abundant return. He is the God of more than enough.

**2 Thessalonians 3:3** – *But the Lord is faithful, and He will strengthen you and protect you from the evil one.* (NIV)

**Hebrews 10:23** – *Let us hold fast the confession of our hope without wavering, for He who promised is faithful.* (NKJV)

Hope is sparked by our faith and can be fanned into a fiery inferno in our heart if we continue to feed its fires. Hope is anchored to God through Christ. Are you living in anticipation of fulfillment of your cherished desire? Are you believing in expectation of your hopes being fulfilled? Are you expecting God's promises to manifest in your life?

Many of us can honestly answer that we are not;

but it is within our power to change that. When we choose to walk in faith, growing closer to God; our hope will grow to greater heights. Do not let fear of disappointment hold you back from feeding your hope. Let your hope grow in the Lord. Ask Him to show up and show out in your life and then sit back and watch in amazement what He will do. Hope in the Lord through Christ leads to a greater love, a Godly love.

**1 Thessalonians 5:8** – *But let us, who are of the day, be sober, putting on the breastplate of faith and love; and for an helmet, the hope of salvation.* (KJV)

**Love:**

**Matthew 22:37-39** - *[37]Jesus said to him, 'You shall love the Lord your God with all your heart, with all your soul, and with all your mind.' [38]This is the first and greatest commandment. [39]And the second is like it: 'You shall love your neighbor as yourself.'* (NKJV)

**1 John 4:16** – *And we have known and believed the love that God has for us. God is love, and he who abides in love abides in God, and God in him.* (NKJV)

**1 John 4:8** – *He who does not love does not know God, for God is love.* (NKJV)

God's greatest commandment to us is to love. Why love? Because God IS love! To love is to know God.

The more you love, the deeper you love, the more unconditional your love becomes; the better you will know God. In fact, scripture specifically says that if you do not know love, you do not know God.

Scripture tells us a lot about love including the fact that without it, we have nothing (**1Corinthians 13:1-3**). Love is the greatest of all God's commandments (**Mark 12:29-31**). Love binds (**Colossians 3:14**). Love covers a multitude of sins (**1 Peter 4:8; Proverbs 10:12**). Love is sacrificial (**John 15:13**). Love casts out fear (**1 John 4:18**). Love is the fruit of the Spirit and promotes the growth of other good fruit (**Galatians 5:22; Ephesians 4:2**). Love is eternal (**1 Corinthians 13:8**).

We love because God first loved us (**1 John 4:19**). Christ was the embodiment of love, including sacrificial love. God loved us so much that He gave His only son so that we may live. Christ loved us so much that He willingly sacrificed His own life to reunite us with the Father. Love abounds in God, and it is listed in the King James Version Bible over four hundred times. That should give you an idea of how important love is to God, and how much He wants us to love Him and ALL His children.

I challenge you to read **1 Corinthians 13:4-10** and see how you see yourself in light of this scripture. Then read it again picturing the verses as they apply to Jesus. This is the reason we should strive to live a more Christ-like life: to be able to love like Jesus loved. The more you love, the more you will develop a heart of Jesus and the closer you will draw to the Lord. Drawing closer to the Lord in love will help you survive the storms of life, sheltered by His love.

**1 Corinthians 13:4-8** – *⁴Love suffers long and is kind; love does not envy; love does not parade itself, is not puffed up: ⁵does not behave rudely, does not seek its own, is not provoked, thinks no evil; ⁶does not rejoice in iniquity, but rejoices in the truth; ⁷bears all things, believes all things, hopes all things, endures all things. ⁸Love never fails. But whether there are prophecies, they will fail; whether there are tongues, they will cease; whether there is knowledge, it will vanish away.* (NKJV)

**1 Thessalonians 1:3** – *We continually remember before our God and Father your work produced by faith, your labor prompted by love, and you endurance inspired by hope in our Lord Jesus Christ.* (NIV)

## Take the I out of Bitter to Get Better

**2 Corinthians 4:16** – *Therefore we do not lose heart. Though outwardly we are wasting away, yet inwardly we are being renewed day by day.* (NIV)

To truly seek God, you have to get out of your own way. It is our nature to be self-absorbed; to be focused on our own needs, desires, hurts, circumstances, problems, etc. But God calls us to leave our old nature behind, to put aside our "selves" and turn our eyes to Him. We often get in our own way in our pursuit of God.

We try to do things in our own self efforts, thinking we know best or God isn't going to care about our insignificant issues. We push forward chasing our own wants instead of asking God what He wants for us. We stew in our own hurts, disappointments, and dissatisfaction fueling the bitterness that grows within us. We put all of these obstacles and stumbling blocks in our own path when seeking God, and then we ask God to remove them.

Identity the issues that you have placed in the way of reaching God and begin removing them one by one.

If it is an area you struggle with removing, ask God to help you. To remove the bitter seeds that have been planted in your life, you have to change how you react to those issues that planted the seeds in the first place and how you think about them.

You can't just complain about your circumstances and expect something to change. That will never promote change. You need to identify what is causing the issue in the first place and take it out at the root.

If the bitterness is a negative reaction to the actions of others, think about what you can change in the situation. You may not be able to stop the behavior because it isn't yours to stop, but you can stop how you react to it. You may have tried addressing the issue with the other person to no avail, but once you have addressed it and it continues to happen; you should remove yourself from the situation, if at all possible. If this isn't possible, then share your situation with another Godly person who can give you wise council.

**Psalms 1:1** – *Blessed is the man who walks not in the counsel of the ungodly, nor stands in the path of sinners, nor sits in the seat of the scornful.* (NKJV)

Who is the Deborah or Solomon in your life, the

wise man or woman with Godly advice you can turn to? That is the person you should go to. If you don't have one, seek out a Christian counselor in your church or community.

**John 14:17** – *"the Spirit of truth, whom the world cannot receive, because it neither sees Him nor knows Him; but you know Him, for He dwells with you and will be in you".* (NKJV)

Whatever advice you are given, take it to the Lord in prayer and ask Him to reveal the truth to you. Also, compare their advice to what the Word says. If it is contradictory to the Word, it is not Godly wisdom but is a lie from the Enemy sent to steal your joy. Once you have turned to the Word, take the issue to God in prayer.

If it is something that you are struggling with being able to let go of or you are holding on to it with resentment, let it go by submitting it to God. Once it is given to God, DO NOT pick it back up. Every time you feel the old emotions rising, go to God again in prayer and supplication and ask that He remove the roots of bitterness from your heart and give you the strength and wisdom to respond to the situation in a Godly manner rather than react in the flesh. To follow God, we have to die to ourselves (to our flesh) daily.

**Luke 9:23** – *Then He said to them all, "If anyone desires to come after Me, let him deny himself, and take up his cross daily, and follow Me."* (NKJV)

Choosing to follow and serve God is a daily decision. We are called to die to our flesh daily. To truly seek and find God, you must die to your old self over and over again. Every day the Enemy will bring parts of our old selves and our old lives to the forefront of our minds. It is our choice whether to pick up the temptation he is presenting or to deny ourselves and die a little more to our flesh.

Our old selves are of the world and we have to renew our minds, our spirits, our hearts, and our souls to become more Christ-like each and every day and to battle the traps and temptations the Enemy has planned for us. God says that He has begun a good work in us that will continue until the day we die. We are called to do our part by letting our old selves (and our past) go and seeking Him in ALL of our ways. Praise and worship God through it all. It is difficult to be bitter or self-absorbed when you are praising and worshipping the Lord.

To truly let go of the past and the ties that bind us in life, we have to give it ALL to God. So often we hold back parts of our heart because it is too painful, too shameful, or too much for us to deal with and we aren't ready to let God have that part. That just hinders us and our progress and healing. We have to purge the past and break the chains that are weighing us down and holding us back from the full life God has planned for us. True life is found through Christ in God.

**Proverbs 8:35** – *For whoever finds me finds life, and obtains favor from the Lord.* (NKJV)

In order to truly be free of those things that hold us back, we have to seek the truth and give it to God. One of the Enemy's greatest weapon is the lies he can get us to believe: lies about ourselves, lies about God, lies about the motivation of others, lies about our past or our circumstances, lies about anything in our lives that he can form into a weapon to use against us. But God says no weapon formed against us shall prosper. He is our defender, our shield and our truth. Bring the issues into the light and submit them to God to take away the power the Enemy has to use them against you.

**Isaiah 54:17** – *"No weapon formed against you shall prosper, and every tongue which rises against you in judgement You shall condemn. This is the heritage of the servants of the Lord, and their righteousness is from Me," says the Lord.* (NKJV)

**Psalms 119:114** – *You are my hiding place and my shield; I hope in Your word.* (NKJV)

# Bring It Into the Light

**Acts 26:18** – *To open their eyes, and to turn them from darkness to light, and from the power of Satan unto God, that they may receive forgiveness of sins, and inheritance among them which are sanctified by faith that is in me.* (KJV)

Take the weapon away from the Enemy by bringing it into the light and submitting it to God. The Enemy tries to keep us in darkness because that is where he has power; but he is powerless against the light of the Lord. He uses our fears, our surroundings, other people, our emotions, circumstances, and any other weapon he can to drag us into the dark.

When we focus on the light, we will make it through the darkness regardless of the Enemy's attacks on us. When we stop focusing on the light and moving toward it, we can become engulfed by the darkness surrounding us and it is much harder to start moving again. When you have some hidden secret or part of your life that you keep in the dark parts of your heart, unwilling to share it with even God, the Enemy uses that as a weapon against you. When you bring it into the light by surrendering it to God, he can heal that broken part of your heart too and can remove the weapon that the Enemy has been using in your life.

I know some things are difficult to talk about and if you can't tell anyone else, that is okay. But you need to give it to God so you can heal from whatever it is. He already knows. There is nothing that is hidden from God. Don't let whatever emotion tied to that hidden part of your heart or life keep you from the full and abundant life God has for you in close fellowship with Him.

**Jeremiah 16:17** – *My eyes are on all their ways; they are not hidden from me, nor is their sin concealed from my eyes.* (NIV)

Victims of abuse, especially sexual abuse, have a very hard time talking about it and because it isn't talked about, it is ignored like it doesn't exist. But it does exist; acting like it doesn't won't make it disappear. It's there, waiting in the darkness to wage the next battle, to pounce on the next victim.

**John 1:5** – *The light shines in the darkness, and the darkness has not overcome it.* (NIV)

If we share our testimonies with others, people will

realize it IS happening and maybe we can battle it together. It helps to know that you are not alone, that someone else has been where you are or truly understands the burdens you carry. If I can share my story and prevent even one person from having to endure what I have lived through, I will gladly bare my whole heart and all its brokenness to the world. If it will make one mother think twice about who they let their children be around or how "adult" they allow them to dress, then I will gladly tell all. The monsters don't see a little girl playing dress up, the monsters see an innocent bird that they can prey upon.

It isn't easy, and it is painful to talk about it; but it's just as painful to keep trying to stuff it all deep down inside and rebuild the shattered wall where it was all hidden. When you build walls like that, the darkness keeps trying to seep through the cracks into the rest of your life. But once you realize it isn't your battle alone and you can give it to God, it makes the load lighter to carry. I don't know about you, but my load through life is heavy enough without carrying around any unnecessary baggage. Some stories need to be told and brought into the light and some people need those stories to be told.

**1 John 4:18** – *"There is no fear in love; but perfect love casts out fear: because fear involves torment. But he who fears has not been made perfect in love.* (NKJV)

**Psalm 89:15** – *Blessed are the people who know the joyful sound! They walk, O Lord, in the light of Your countenance.* (NKJV)

# Lighten Your Load

**Matthew 11:28-30** – *28Then Jesus said, "Come to me, all of you who are weary and carry heavy burdens, and I will give you rest. 29Take my yoke upon you. Let me teach you, because I am humble and gentle at heart, and you will find rest for your souls. 30For my yoke is easy to bear, and the burden I give you is light."* (NLT)

Whatever load you might be carrying, whatever skeletons are living in your closet, whatever hidden burdens are weighing you down, whatever broken parts of your heart you are holding on to; I encourage you to bring it into the light and give it to God. It is only going to continue to hold you back from the abundant life God has planned for you.

I saw a church marquee once that said, "God heals broken hearts, but you have to give Him all the pieces". How true that is. We ask God to heal our broken hearts, but then we hold back pieces to ourselves and don't want to turn it over to His gentle healing. It makes me think of a small child who has a splinter in their foot. As soon as "mom" pulls out the needle, the freak out commences. They don't want you to touch it because it hurts and they are afraid you are going to make it hurt worse. Half the time they are still wailing after the obtrusion is removed.

Aren't we the same way, saying "No God, it hurts too much"? But God is oh so gentle and knows exactly how to fix our brokenness. We just have to be willing to turn it over to him. Allow God's light to shine on your brokenness, give Him your whole heart, and watch the amazing healing He will perform in your life.

**Psalm 147:3** – *He heals the brokenhearted and binds up their wounds.* (NKJV)

**Psalm 34:18** – *The Lord is close to the brokenhearted and saves those who are crushed in spirit.* (NIV)

Often those hidden broken parts of our hearts were caused by sin: either our own or the sins of others afflicted against us. Whether we hold it back out of guilt, shame, hurt, bitterness, unforgiveness, anger, resentment, fear or any other negative emotion tied to it; we have to be willing to face it and give it to God to get better, to become whole once more. You have to have faith and let go of the past, the hurt, the betrayals, the brokenness…. give it all to God and you will be amazed at what He can make out of it. If God says He remembers your sins no more (and the sins of others) why do you continue to remember them?

**Psalm 103:12** – *As far as the east is from the west, so far has He removed our transgressions from us.* (NKJV)

**Hebrews 8:12** – *"For I will be merciful to their unrighteousness, and their sins and their lawless deeds I will remember no more."* (NKJV)

**1 Peter 5:7** – *Cast all your anxiety on Him because He cares for you.* (NIV)

This sounds so simple and so cliché: just give it to God. It really is that simple but it isn't that simple to do. It takes a humble heart, a willingness to forgive and submit to God's greater authority, and a level of faith and trust in God and His grace that we often fall short of ever reaching on our own. There are so many things in our lives that we need to give to God: our hurt, our shortcomings, our sins, our betrayals, our fears, our insecurities, the lies the Enemy has sold us, our shame, our bitterness, our shattered and broken selves, even our thoughts and ideas.

When we give these burdens to God, He makes a wonderful exchange with us. The God who takes our old stained, world weary soul and gives us a clean, vibrant, forgiven, sin-free self in return is a truly magnificent and merciful Father. Imagine what wonderful things He will exchange for the other parts we are reluctant to give Him.

**Psalm 55:22** – *Cast your burden on the Lord, and He shall sustain you; He shall never permit the righteous to be moved.* (NKJV)

**Philippians 3:13** – *Brothers, I do not consider myself yet to have taken hold of it. But one thing I do: Forgetting what is behind and straining toward what is ahead.* (NIV)

## Tend Your Garden

In life, sometimes you are the Sower, sometimes you are the Grower and sometimes you are the Spectator. A sower is a person who is planting seeds in the ground to grow. There will be people throughout your life that you are the one who is sowing the seeds in their life. It may be someone that you gave a bit of Godly advice to, it may be your children or your spouse or it may be someone that you never realized you had affected in any way.

**Hosea 10:12** – *Sow for yourself righteousness; reap in mercy, break up your fallow ground, for it is time to seek the Lord, till He comes and rains righteousness on you.* (NKJV)

We often plant seeds in others' lives without ever realizing it. They can be good seeds or bad seeds depending on how we interact with that person. When we are kind, considerate, compassionate, forgiving, loving, and understanding to others, treating them in a Christ-like manner; we are sowing good seeds. When we treat others harshly, being unkind, selfish, cruel, hateful or hurtful; we are sowing bad seeds in their lives. It is up to us what type of seed we choose to sow. Remember that we reap whatever we sow, so sow mindfully.

**Galatians 6:7** – *Do not be deceived, God is not mocked; for whatever a man sows, the he will also reap.* (NKJV)

**2 Corinthians 9:6** – *But this I say: He who sows sparingly will also reap sparingly, and he who sows bountifully will also reap bountifully.* (NKJV)

**James 3:18** – *Now the fruit of righteousness is sown in peace by those who make peace.* (NKJV)

A grower would be someone who helps the crop to grow by supplying good nutrients, water, sunlight and care. There are many people who come in your life for a season (or a lifetime) for you to help cultivate the good crops in their lives or for them to nourish the crops in your life. These may be friends, family, co-workers or others who you show care for or who care for you.

When you allow toxic emotions and reactions to others to grow in your garden or foster that growth in others' gardens by being the infestation of nastiness in their garden; you are allowing the Enemy to kill the good growth, steal the loving nourishment, and destroy the crops of good fruit.

You determine what you allow in your garden and what you bring into the gardens of others. I encourage you to be a grower when tending others' gardens, you will be amazed by the good fruit God will allow to grow under your watchful eye.

**Matthew 12:33** – *"Either make the tree good and its fruit good, or else make the tree bad and its fruit bad; for a tree is known by its fruit."* (NKJV)

A spectator is someone who is observing, sitting back and watching the circumstances of others. They are generally not taking an active part but have a more passive role. When my children became adults, I became more of a spectator in their lives. I was still a part of their lives but in more of a peripheral way than being at the center of their lives like when they were growing up.

This is a normal part of life but it is sometimes difficult for us as parents to realize that we are no longer responsible for their growth. We have moved from the role of grower to spectator. As a spectator, we are watching the growth occur but are often not actively involved.

Our role may move from spectator to grower or even sower. Sometimes we are a spectator for our own good and sometimes we are a spectator for the good of others. God may use us as witnesses of His great wonders and mercies in the growth of others. There are times when it is difficult for us to accept our role as spectators when we want to be an active part in the process, but be patient and wait upon the Lord to show you when to be active and when to wait and observe in patient obedience. Ask God to show you where He would have you sow, grow, watch, or harvest in the various areas of your lives.

**2 Peter 1:16 –** *For we did not follow cleverly invented stories when we told you about the power and coming of our Lord Jesus Christ, but we were eyewitnesses of his majesty.* (NIV)

Regardless of what season of life you are in, be thankful for the sprouts. We always want to see the seeds in our lives bear fruit right away but just like seeds planted in a garden, it takes time for the seed to grow. The more good nutrients it receives the faster it will grow; but the bigger the plant, the longer it will need to grow and the stronger it will become over time. It is important that it develops strong roots so it isn't destroyed in the first storm of life it encounters.

There are trees, such as a Cottonwood tree, which grow very quickly; but it is also a very soft wooded tree and will be taken down easier than a tree that grew more slowly over time. It is considered a poorer type of wood as it rots quickly. A giant Redwood in comparison may live over a thousand years and grows to great heights. It is slower growing, but it is extremely tall and strong.

We often overlook the small things including the small beginnings, but we should be thankful for the sprouts in our lives and be patient and diligent in providing proper nourishment to encourage future growth and to reap the harvest of good fruit. Everything has to start somewhere and God is a master at making something out of seemingly nothing. Remember that faith as small as a mustard seed can move mountains.

**Zechariah 4:10** – *"Do not despise these small beginnings, for the Lord rejoices to see the work begin, to see the plumb line in Zerubbabel's hand."* (NLT)

You also have to continually grow in Christian life. If you don't grow, you will become stagnant. Stagnant is defined by Webster as "not flowing", "to become stale or foul from standing", "to stop developing, growing, progressing, or advancing", and "to become sluggish or dull". Have you ever looked at a small body of water that has no movement or fresh water added to it?

If you have, you probably noticed that over time; the water turns from clear, pure water to murky water you can't see through, with algae and bacteria growing in it and becomes a haven for parasites and pests like mosquitoes. It not only looks foul, but it begins to smell foul too.

Think about a fish tank that doesn't have any circulation or filter. It quickly becomes cloudy and slimy. If left that way for too long, the fish will die from the filth. The fish need clean water with oxygen and other life-giving components that are destroyed by the murk in the water. On a regular basis, you have to remove some of the dirty water to make room for fresh, clean water; vacuum out the nastiness that settles in the cracks and crevices; and provide a nurturing environment to promote growth. The same is true in our lives.

Have you been just sitting in your own filthy water, not seeking to remove the dirt or add fresh water? Our souls and spiritual life can be that murky pool of water, full of filth and becoming a breeding ground for parasites if we don't remove some of the dirt, cultivate the soil and add good nutrients, make room for the living water, and promote growth. Use God's Word to purify your life and as a filter for the impurities that try to take root.

**Proverbs 30:5** – *Every word of God is pure; He is a shield to those who put their trust in Him.* (NKJV)

From time to time, you have to pull the weeds in your garden. Webster defines a weed as "a plant that is not valued where it is growing and is usually of vigorous growth; one that tends to overgrow or choke out more desirable plants" or "an obnoxious growth, thing or person". Whether it is in a flower bed, a vegetable garden or a field of crops; the weeds need to be pulled to allow growth for the good seeds.

The weeds of life, like the weeds in a garden, are faster growing than the good crops and if you aren't careful, they can quickly overrun your garden and become deeply rooted there. The weeds will drop seed for more weeds to grow; they grow faster and can choke out the good crops; grow deep and strong root systems so they are difficult to eradicate; and they steal the nutrients, sunlight, and water needed to sustain life for the good crops.

Pulling the weeds in your life may be a daily task in some seasons. It seems as if you just cultivated your garden and suddenly it is being invaded by weeds. But when we are too busy worrying about the weeds in our neighbors' gardens and not tending our own gardens, that's when the weeds REALLY take over. Tending our own garden will keep us too busy to worry about what our neighbor is growing in their gardens or how their garden is growing.

Weeds, like the Enemy, only come to steal and kill and destroy. They must be pulled before they take strong root, kill our good growth, and are more difficult to remove. What weeds are you allowing to grow in your garden?

I often pray that God will remove the weeds from my heart, those things that I may not even know have taken root there but are keeping the good seeds from growing well. Identify the weeds and bad seeds that you have been cultivating in your garden and the bad fruit that has grown in your life.

Don't compare your garden and your path to that of other believers (or non-believers). We are each called to grow OUR garden and there may be fruit in our garden that no one else is able to grow in theirs. If we don't take up the task, that fruit and the person it is meant for may never develop.

We often compare our own relationship with God to that of fellow Christians. Comparison is a huge and deadly weed if allowed to take root in your garden. Don't get discouraged because Susie talks about how she hears from God or how God told her this or that. This is about your walk with God, not Susie's.

Never let anyone else (or yourself) make you feel like you are not enough or you can't have a strong relationship with the Lord. That is a lie from the King of Liars and I rebuke it!

There is only one way to get to God but there are lots of paths leading to that one way. The walk someone else is taking is their walk, not yours. Just as we are each uniquely made, the way we communicate with God and sense His presence in our life is unique to our individual circumstances, our Spiritual Gifts, and God's calling on our lives.

There isn't a perfect recipe to finding God. Scripture says, if you seek Him, you will find Him. Seek Him in the way that is true to who you are, and you will make it. Sometimes in our walk with God, we must start out on our knees and crawl before we can stand up and walk. And that's okay because the best way to find God is on our knees.

**Ephesians 3:14** – *For this reason I bow my knees to the Father of our Lord Jesus Christ.* (NKJV)

# Give It Time

**Psalm 147:3** – *He heals the brokenhearted and bandages their wounds.* (NLT)

Healing takes time. I disagree with the old saying that time heals all wounds because some wounds are too deep to ever truly heal; but time does lessen the pain and with God's help, most wounds can be healed even if they leave some scars behind.

Everything in life has seasons: the year is divided into four seasons; the world goes through seasons of war, seasons of peace, seasons of drought, seasons of prosperity; and our own lives go through many seasons. Each person's seasons may be different from the next persons because we are each unique and have very different life experiences, upbringing, beliefs, and back-grounds. But we all go through seasons.

There will be seasons of strife, seasons of abundant blessings, seasons of loss, seasons of hope, seasons of loneliness, seasons of love and joy. There are so many seasons that each of us go through during our lives.

If you are going through a difficult season in your life, find hope in the fact that whatever you are going through is just for a set time or a season. It is not a permanent placement. However, how long we are in a season often depends on how we react to it. If we live in worry and negativity, the bad seasons are likely to draw out; but if we turn our negative situations over to God and push through the storm in continuous prayer, God will bring us into a better season. After every winter or dry season, there is almost always a season of spring on the other side with new growth and beauty waiting there.

**Ecclesiastes 3:1-8** – *¹There is a time for everything, and a season for every activity under the heavens: ²a time to be born and a time to die, a time to plant and a time to uproot; ³a time to kill and a time to heal, a time to tear down and a time to build; ⁴a time to weep and a time to laugh, a time to mourn and a time to dance; ⁵a time to scatter stones and a time to gather them, a time to embrace and a time to refrain; ⁶a time to search and a time to give up, a time to keep and a time to throw away; ⁷a time to tear and a time to mend, a time to be silent and a time to speak; ⁸a time to love and a time to hate, a time for war and a time for peace.* (NIV)

Some wounds are much deeper than others and will take a longer time to heal. My son was a wrestler in Junior High and High School. He was on the shorter side (poor kid inherited my height and grey hair), but he was a fierce wrestler. He may have been smaller than the other guys but he put his whole heart and determination into wrestling his opponent and would often slither out from any hold they had on him.

The weekend of his fourteenth birthday, he had a wrestling tournament at school, from Friday through Sunday. On Saturday, between matches, he came up to me in the stands and told me his knee hurt. It was swollen and had a small pimple like spot over his knee cap. I told him to talk to his coach about it. The coach told him it was inflamed from being on it so much during his matches and to keep it elevated and put ice on it when he wasn't on the mat. He continued wrestling in the tournament all weekend, regardless of the pain and swelling in his knee.

Monday afternoon I received a call from one of his Wrestling Coaches telling me that he had a severe staph infection and I needed to take him to the doctor. He wasn't allowed to return to school until the staph infection was completely healed. What looked like a small spot on his knee hid a greater wound under the surface.

The coach told me he had squeezed out a ton of infection from the wound, and my son needed to go to the doctor right away. It was late in the afternoon so we went to an Urgent Care facility and lucky for us there was a wound care nurse on staff that night. She said that the infection was deep and had already started eating away the skin from the inside, and my son would need to come every day for a week to get it cleaned and remove any new infection.

She took a sample of the infected tissue to verify it was not a more serious infection called MRSA (methicillin-resistant staphylococcus aureus). I knew little about staph or MRSA other than it wasn't good; was easily transferred and spread; was a skin infection that affected the deep tissue; and once you have it, you are more likely to get it again.

Every evening for a week, I would go pick up my son and take him to see the wound care nurse. I sat by his side, watching as she squeezed his knee so hard the skin around it turned purple and white; my son gripping the sides of the gurney so hard, I thought he would bend the metal to keep from crying out in pain. He was so brave and so strong through it all, but I could tell it was extremely painful.

She had to remove all the infection so it would not continue to fester and spread. She would squeeze and push the infection out from this direction and that until nothing but clear fluid was coming from the wound, then she would rinse it out with a saline solution (which probably hurt like the dickens too), and pack the wound and wrap it until we came back the next day. She marked the furthest red mark on his leg with a marker, so we could tell if the infection spread from the day before and we had to watch that he didn't have any other lesions on his skin anywhere.

I remember on the second or third day, you could see straight down to the bone in his leg from the open wound once it was cleansed. It was a terrible thing to have to watch my son endure, knowing there was nothing I could do to make the process any easier or less painful for him; knowing I would have to bring him back the next day and do it all over again. But the alternative was so much worse. Letting the wound continue to fester could have cost him his leg or his life.

The infection had to be taken out before it could do any more damage.

Some of the wounds in our heart are like my son's staph infection. They may seem like they are healed on the surface but hiding beneath the surface is a massive infection turning septic in our hearts and our minds. It eats away at our flesh from the inside out; poisoning our bodies, our minds, our hearts and even our souls. God is like that wound care nurse. He does it much more gently than she did, but He knows what is best for us and He knows that poison has to come out for us to heal.

God will treat the wound so very gently, but He will continue to try to gain access to that most painful part because He knows He has the ultimate cure. He will lance open the wound even though it is painful. He shares that pain with us; going through it all, right beside us, holding our hand saying, "I know My child, let Me help you. Trust Me, it is for your best".

He cleanses the wound from the inside out, but knows that if He takes it all at once, it will leave a gaping hole behind; a hole that may allow other things to come in or will cause greater pain. Instead, He removes the painful tissue of the wounds one layer at a time, gently removing one layer so His light can reach the next, deeper, more painful layer and let His healing light in for deeper healing.

Once the infection is completely removed by God, the good growth can develop in its place with new things God has for you; your heart can heal, your life can be restored, your love can begin again. God plants new seeds behind in the hollow ground left by the open wound. He very gently covers the dirt over the new seeds planted there, waters it, feeds it, and says, "Trust me. You will see better growth coming".

But He had to remove all of the darkness, all of the festering wounds, all of the poison, all of the dead tissue, all of the rotting weeds to promote new growth. He can heal the most broken pieces and the worst infections (addiction, suffering, depression, strongholds), but we have to be willing to give it over to Him for His healing grace. It will most likely not be instantly healed (but it may), but God will heal it. Give it time and let God in.

They say the definition of insanity is doing the same thing over and over again and expecting different results. In life we do that, we get comfortable where we are and feel like we can live with the pain we know better than the pain of the unknown. Sometimes our comfort zone needs to be broken. God is a God of more than enough, and that calls us to be stretched and to continually grow and not become stagnant. Sometimes He has to clean away what is left behind by the fires; the residue, the ash, the festering wounds.

That means we have to change and be willing to change. We have to change the way we look at things; we have to be understanding and accepting of one another; respecting each other's boundaries; and be willing to push a little bit when we need to….push back a little bit when something is too hard or when someone is asking us to do something that is too painful or pushing forward through the storm.

You will need to be willing to tell the other person "that hurts, please stop". You don't have to be rude or angry, just verbal. Their truth is not your truth. Truth is truth, that is true; but we each have a very unique perspective based on our beliefs, our experiences, our life, and sometimes on the lies the Enemy has sold us. Be willing to shift your perspective. It is like looking through a kaleidoscope: if you turn it a little bit, the whole picture changes. But it is always beautiful, ever changing with beautiful colors shining through...not bad, just different. Allow God to heal your wounds and change your perspective.

## Be Still and Let God Be God

**Psalm 46:10-11** – [10]*"Be still, and know that I am God;
I will be exalted among the nations; I will be exalted in
the earth."* [11]*The Lord hosts is with us; the God of
Jacob is our refuge. Selah* (NCV)

It's okay to not be okay. In fact, God knows that
we are not going to be okay sometimes, and He's okay
with that. He tells us to "Be still and know that I am
God". This verse always speaks to my heart. It tells me
it's okay for me to not always know what to do; it's
okay for me to feel broken; it's okay for me to just stop,
take a time out and just BE STILL and let God's will be
done.

A lot of times, we are so busy trying to make
something happen, trying to do the "right" thing, trying
to survive this roller coaster ride called life; that we
forget to just sit down on the side lines and let God do
His thing. He really doesn't need our help.

God will let us know when it is time to act and
which direction to go, but He will also let us sit out
some parts and not try so hard. He's got this! Just let
Him work and be amazed at the perfection and timing
of His plan when you see the whole thing laid out

before you.

You will almost NEVER see what He is up to in the midst of the storm. You have to walk through it with faith and trust and be awed by the beauty waiting on the other side that is like nothing you could have possibly imagined for yourself.

**Matthew 9:29** – *Then he touched their eyes and said, "According to your faith, will it be done to you."* (NIV)

**Isaiah 40:31** – *But they that wait upon the Lord shall renew their strength; they shall mount up with wings as eagles; they shall run, and not be weary; and they shall walk, and not faint.* (KJV)

There are over twenty-five times when the Bible says, "be still". The most well-known is the verse listed above. Many of the greatest victories in the Bible occurred after the person stood still and leaned on God, and waited upon the Lord. Naomi tells Ruth to stand still (**Ruth 3:18**), Samuel told Saul to stand still (**1Samuel 9:27**), Job says that he stands still before the Lord (**Job 3:13**), and Jesus told the stormy winds to "be still" on the Sea of Galilee (**Mark 4:39**).

We are often called to "be still" before the Lord and before the raging storms in our life while God goes about His good works. We are to stand still in faith, lean into the Lord, and grow through the adversities against us. When you do not know what else to do, be still and turn to the Lord. Wait in patience on the Lord, then be obedient to what He tells you to do.

**2 Chronicles 20:17** – '*You will not need to fight in this battle. Position yourselves, stand still and see the salvation of the Lord, who is with you, O Judah and Jerusalem!' Do not fear or be dismayed; tomorrow go out against them, for the Lord is with you.* (NKJV)

**Psalms 46:10** – *Be still, and know that I am God; I will be exalted among the nations, I will be exalted in the earth!* (NKJV)

## A Beautiful Exchange

When you make the choice to follow God, accept salvation through Jesus Christ by asking for forgiveness and receiving Christ into your heart and the Holy Spirit dwells inside you; there is a beautiful exchange that begins to occur. First, God makes you a new creation in Him. God exchanges your temporary earthly existence for a beautifully blessed eternal life.

**1 Peter 1:23** – *You have been born again, and this new life did not come from something that dies but from something that cannot die. You were born again through God's living message that continues forever.* (NCV)

If you have not asked Christ into your life, I humbly ask that you take a moment now and determine if this is a choice you would like to make. I pray that everyone becomes saved and enjoys the more abundant life that God has for them, but it is a choice you must make for yourself. No one else can make it for you. If you feel you are ready to make this choice and begin the beautiful exchange, below is a simple prayer you can say and mean with your entire heart to become the new you in Christ. Ask God to give you the words to speak if you are unsure of what to say.

*Father God, I humbly come before you today. I know that I am a sinner and I confess my sins before you. I ask in Jesus' Name that You will forgive me of all my sins. I give my heart and my life to You this day, Lord. Your Word says that if I believe in my heart and confess with my mouth that Jesus Christ is Lord, the one who died for me and was raised again by the Father, that I will be saved. I believe with my whole heart and I speak this confession that Jesus is Lord and Savior of my life. I choose this day to serve You Lord and to follow Your ways. Make in me a clean heart Father and make me a new creation in You. I thank You and praise You for all You are and all You do. In Jesus' Name I pray, Amen.*

**Romans 10:9-10 –** *[9]That if you confess with your mouth "Jesus is Lord", and believe in your heart that God raised Him from the dead, you will be saved. [10]For it is with your heart that you believe and are justified, and it is with your mouth that you confess and are saved.* (NIV)

**Acts 2:21** *– 'And it shall come to pass that whoever calls on the name of the Lord shall be saved.'* (NKJV)

**Philippians 2:11 –** *and that every tongue should confess that Jesus Christ is Lord, to the glory of God the Father.* (NKJV)

Second, God exchanges your broken world-worn heart for a new heart. God exchanges our broken, battered, and bruised heart which has been hardened by life for a fresh new, clean, pure heart. At the same time, He gives us a new spirit and renews our minds. God knows that we have stained our soul and spirit with sin, we have had our hearts broken and allowed bitter seeds to grow in our heart, we have allowed our minds to be filled with the toxic things of the world instead of the pure things of God.

God exchanges our world-weary ones for His newly cleaned and heavenly minded ones. It is a beautiful exchange, and we always come out better in our exchanges with the Lord. Have faith and trust in the good gifts He has for you. He wants you to have a more abundant life, and He knows how to give us the good desires of our hearts. True happiness and joy come from God.

**Ezekiel 36:26** – *I will give you a new heart and put a new spirit within you; I will take the heart of stone out of your flesh and give you a heart of flesh.* (NKJV)

**Ezekiel 11:19** – *Then I will give them one heart, and I will put a new spirit within them, and take the stony heart out of their flesh, and give them a heart of flesh.* (NKJV)

**Romans 12:2** – *Do not conform any longer to the pattern of this world, but be transformed by the renewing of your mind. Then you will be able to test and approve what God's will is – His good, pleasing and perfect will.* (NIV)

**Psalm 51:10** – *Create in me a clean heart, O God, and renew a steadfast spirit within me.* (NKJV)

**Ephesians 4:23 –** *And be renewed in the spirit of your mind.* (KJV)

## Satan Is a Liar

**John 10:10 -** *"The thief does not come except to steal, and to kill, and to destroy. I have come that they may have life, and that they may have it more abundantly"* (NKJV)

Satan is a liar and a thief. He will kill your joy, he will steal your hope, and he will destroy your relationships. He is the Enemy and he knows the best weapons to use against you. He knows exactly what our insecurities are, what our weaknesses are, and he knows the Word. After all, he began in Heaven as one of God's Holy Angels.

He can slither into your thoughts so seamlessly that you will not even realize that he is the one planting that seed of dissention, the root of envy, the weeds in your thoughts that are trying to choke out the Godly crops in your life. He knows us so well, that we often do not realize how he is using our own thoughts, doubts, fears, insecurities, weaknesses, hurt, past, disappointments and circumstances against us.

There is a reason that he was represented as a serpent in the Garden of Eden. When I was a little girl, I remember walking in our back pasture to the pig pen with my parents and some family. The grass was tall and as I was trailing along behind my parents, I stepped on something that I thought was a big stick. It was actually a very large snake lying in the grass that I hadn't seen. Fortunately, it slithered away without striking but it left me with an irrational fear of snakes. None of us realized it was there because it was so low to the ground, like Satan it was hidden in plain sight just out of our vision.

As you can tell, we lived in the country when I was young. We would find snakes curled up in the chicken coop eating the eggs, in the bags of animal feed, and at times inside the house. The snakes were able to get in to places where they shouldn't be through the cracks and crevices, because they can flatten themselves and slither in through the small openings. The Enemy does the same. He will find any crack or space he can use to infiltrate your life through others, through your own thoughts and through your circumstances. So, how do you keep him at bay?

Just like in sports, the best defense is a good offense. Let God be your defense by filling in those gaps with His Word, your prayer life, and focusing (meditating) on the things of God. Does that mean the Enemy will let up? No way. He doesn't like to lose, and he knows that in the end he will ALWAYS lose; so, he fights us as hard as he can.

When I feel especially under attack by the Enemy, I find hope in God's Word that He will be our defender, our strong tower, and we are safe under His wing. I also began to realize the only reason Satan would be attacking me was if he saw me as a threat. You don't attack someone that isn't a threat to you. This made me realize that when I was under attack, I needed to draw closer to God not only for his protection and guidance, but also because He obviously had something planned in my life that the Enemy was trying to stop. I needed to draw closer so I could be ready when it was my turn to go out onto the field, just like a Coach will call over the next team member he is going to send out to play. Put me in Coach! I am ready!

**Proverbs 18:10** – *The name of the Lord is a strong tower; the righteous run to it and are safe.* (NKJV)

**Psalm 5:12** – *For You, O Lord, will bless the righteous; with favor You will surround him as with a shield.* (NKJV)

## Master Manipulator

In a particularly difficult period in one of my relationships, a person I loved very deeply believed the lies and manipulations of another person and it drove us apart. For several months, my loved one cut me completely out of their life and wouldn't even talk to me. I couldn't understand what had happened or how the situation became so toxic so quickly. This individual knew me better than anyone else and knew who I was as a person, but they believed the lies of this other person and hardened their heart to me.

During this dark period, my loved one did some very hurtful things to me: things that I couldn't believe they would ever do, things that caused deep wounds and heartache, things that I didn't deserve, things that could have destroyed me if not for my lifeline and faith in God. The most painful part to deal with was the fact that this person, whom I loved so much, believed such terrible things about me. In ways, it made me doubt who I was as a person and certainly made me begin to question how others saw me. If this individual who knew me best could believe this about me, was that my hidden self?

The things I was accused of doing could only have been done by a very vengeful and unbalanced person. They were so far out of my nature and who I am, that the accusations were almost ludicrous. But because this individual believed these manipulations, they made some extreme choices during that period which caused greater damage to us both. Many years later my loved one explained that the person who had turned them against me would include enough truth in the lies to make it seem completely believable.

This person was a master manipulator and that is what Satan does to us. He manipulates the truth of our own circumstances (preying on our weaknesses and doubts) to make us believe the lies that he is telling us. He whispers, "God could never forgive you for the things you have done", because he knows we feel that we are unforgivable. He slyly says, "God doesn't love you", because he knows we think that we are unlovable and have been rejected by those we have loved in our lives. He will use the people in your life to fuel your insecurities through their abusive words and lies that you begin to believe.

When you find yourself believing the manipulations of the Enemy, ask God to show you the truth. If it is lies about yourself, ask God how He sees you and look up scriptures on who God says you are. God cannot lie and the truth is found in Him. Combat the Enemy's lies with the truth. The truth will always set you free.

**John 8:32** – *And ye shall know the truth, and the truth shall make you free.* (KJV)

## Who God Says You Are

- You are made in God's image. From the very beginning, we were made to be images of God in this world, to reflect who He is.

  **Genesis 1:27** – *So God created man in His own image, in the image of God he created him; male and female he created them.* (KJV)

- You are "fearfully and wonderfully made".

  **Psalm 139:14** – *I will praise You, for I am fearfully and wonderfully made; marvelous are Your works, and that my soul knows very well.* (NKJV)

- You are made by God.

  **Isaiah 64:8** – *But now, O Lord, You are our Father; we are the clay, and you our potter; and all we are the work of Your hand.* (NKJV)

  **Job 33:4** – *The Spirit of God has made me, and the breath of the Almighty gives me life.* (NKJV)

  **Ephesians 2:10** – *For we are His workmanship, created in Christ Jesus for good works, which God prepared beforehand that we should walk in them.* (NKJV)

- You are holy and blameless.

  **Ephesians 1:4-5** – *4just as He chose us in Him before the foundation of the world, that we should be holy and without blame before Him in love, 5having predestined us to adoption as sons by Jesus Christ to Himself, according to the good pleasure of His will.* (NKJV)

- You are valued by God.

  **Matthew 10:30-31 –** *[30]But the very hairs of your head are all numbered. [31]Do not fear therefore; you are of more value than many sparrows.* (NKJV)

- You are chosen by God.

  **John 15:16** – *You did not choose Me, but I chose you and appointed you that you should go and bear fruit, and that your fruit should remain, that whatever you ask the Father in My name He may give you.* (NKJV)

  **1 Peter 2:9 –** *But you are a chosen generation, a royal priesthood, a holy nation, His own special people, that you may proclaim the praises of Him who called you out of darkness into His marvelous light.* (NKJV)

- You are led by God and held in His hand.

  **Psalm 139:10** – *Even there shall thy hand lead me, and thy right hand shall hold me.* (KJV)

- You are a victor.

  **Romans 8:37 –** *Yet in all these things we are more than conquerors through Him who loved us.* (NKJV)

- You are a friend of Jesus Christ.

  **John 15:15 –** *No longer do I call you servants, for a servant does not know what his master is doing; but I have called you friends, for all things that I have heard from My Father I have made known to you.* (NKJV)

- You are healed.

  **1 Peter 2:24** – *who Himself bore our sins in His own body on the tree, that we, having died to sins, might live for righteousness – by whose stripes you were healed.* (NKJV)

- You have eternal life and are a citizen of Heaven.

  **1 John 5:11** – *And this is the testimony: that God has given us eternal life, and this life is in His Son.* (NKJV)

  **Philippians 3:20** – *For our citizenship is in heaven, from which we also eagerly wait for the Savior, the Lord Jesus Christ.* (NKJV)

- You are righteous.

  **2 Corinthians 5:21** – *For He made Him who knew no sin to be sin for us, that we might become the righteousness of God in Him.* (NKJV)

- You are loved.

  **1 John 4:10** – *Herein is love, not that we loved God, but that He loved us, and sent His Son to be the propitiation for our sins.* (KJV)

- You are redeemed and forgiven.

  **Ephesians 1:7** – *In Him we have redemption through His blood, the forgiveness of sins, according to the riches of His grace.* (NKJV)

## Derail Your Train of Thought

Our thoughts are often like a runaway train, growing momentum and a life of their own, speeding through our mind around sharp turns and through some very dark tunnels and along the edge of the cliffs. Derail that train before it gets away from you.

I know it is hard to believe, but you can control your thoughts. It's easy for people to say, "just don't think about it"; but it's not so easy to do. Thinking about it is often part of the healing process. Dwelling on it, however, is not.

One of the biggest issues in our thinking is that when we are faced with a painful thought we often do one of two things: we dwell on it and obsess over it or we push it away by intentionally thinking about something else or putting it behind that wall of untouchable things in our mind and heart. Neither of these are healthy options and provide an opportunity for the Enemy to use those thoughts as weapons against us.

So how do you deal with the runaway train of thought fueled by your out of control emotions? Submit it to God. God can always line it back on track and get it back under control. So, how do you submit it to God? First go to God in earnest prayer, tell Him what you are struggling with, and ask Him to take the burden from you if you are not meant to bear it. Then ask Him to help you through the issue and show you what you are to learn from it so you can make it through the darkened tunnel and back out into the light without mass destruction.

Second, stop fueling your out of control thoughts by dwelling on the situation and letting your emotions drive the train. When you find yourself thinking about it, tell yourself to stop. Ask God why it is coming back to your mind and what you need to pray about the situation, and then let it go.

Turn your mind to "things above", focusing on what is true and praiseworthy, lovely and admirable; think about those things. Your positive thoughts take the power away from the Enemy. He hates to see you turn your thoughts to God when he has overtaken your thought train. Take control away from him and give it to God where it belongs.

There were times when I would have to stop my runaway thoughts every few minutes, but it became easier with time. Each time I submitted it to God, I grew stronger and more in control of my emotions. If you are really struggling, listen to praise and worship music and praise God through the stormy thoughts. Nothing brings light into the situation faster than praising the Lord.

**Philippians 4:8** – *Finally, brethren, whatever things are true, whatever things are noble, whatever things are just, whatever things are pure, whatever things are lovely, whatever things are of good report – if there is any virtue and if there is anything praiseworthy – meditate on these things.* (NKJV)

**Colossians 3:2** – *Set your mind on things above, not on things on the earth.* (NKJV)

**Matthew 22:37** – *Jesus said to him, "You shall love the Lord your God with all your heart, with all your soul, and with all your mind."* (NKJV)

**Philippians 4:7** – *and the peace of God, which surpasses all understanding, will guard your hearts and minds through Christ Jesus.* (NKJV)

Once you are on the way to getting your thoughts under control, you might also consider what you allow to come out of your mouth. Many of us fail to engage the filter between our brains and our tongues and speak thoughtlessly to others or even to ourselves.

Once a word is spoken, it cannot be retracted. It is out there, and it has power. Words can cut deeper than any sharply honed weapon ever could. God tells us very clearly to guard our words. Jesus said he who has ears to hear, let him hear; he who has eyes to see, let him see. It doesn't say he who has a mouth to speak, let him speak for a reason. We have only one mouth but we often engage it more frequently (and let it get us into more trouble), than our two ears and two eyes.

Before you speak, make sure it is not going to cause harm to you or others. I frequently react without really thinking about what I am going to say or should say. I have inadvertently caused deep pain to my loved ones with my careless words and sometimes with my intentionally heartless ones (words spoken out of pain, desperation, resentment and anger).

I have learned to pray that God would "set a guard over my mouth" and keep locked the door of my lips. Think about a time when something someone said cut you to the quick, then think about a time when you caused pain to another with your words. I would much rather use my tongue to bring healing to others and ask the Holy Spirit to speak through me than to allow my tongue to have free reign inflicting harm to others.

**Psalm 141:3** – *Set a guard, O Lord, over my mouth; keep watch over the door of my lips.* (NKJV)

**Ephesians 4:29** – *Do not let any unwholesome talk come out of your mouths, but only what is helpful for building others up according to their needs, that it may benefit those who listen.* (NIV)

**Matthew 10:20** – *for it will not be you speaking, but the Spirit of your Father speaking through you.* (NIV)

**Psalm 19:14** – *Let the words of my mouth and the meditation of my heart be acceptable in Your sight, O Lord, my strength and my Redeemer.* (NKJV)

**Proverbs 12:18** – *The words of the reckless pierce like swords, but the tongue of the wise brings healing.* (NIV)

# Hidden Idols

Beware of the hidden idols in your life. In a popular reality show, hidden idols are to be sought out and can provide safety, immunity, and a blessing. That is not true of the idols in our lives. It is easy to say, "I don't have any idols. I don't worship other gods.".

Just because we do not worship false gods or statues, that does not mean there are no idols in our lives. Webster defines an idol as "an image or representation of a god used as an object of worship". Okay, I don't worship another god. One commandment down, nine to go.

However, Webster further defines an idol as "a person or thing that is greatly admired, loved, or revered". Alright, so is there any person or thing that I greatly admire, love, or revere that might be coming before God in my life?

For most of us, we can answer with a resounding YES. In the never-ending hustle and bustle of daily survival and juggling act of balancing our lives and overpacked schedules, God is often put on the back burner in our lives.

He becomes an afterthought instead of the main focus. The hidden idol in your life may be your career, money, personal goals, luxuries, video games, your children, your spouse or anything else that you put in your thoughts and time before God. God is to come first in your life and everything else will fall into place. What is your hidden idol?

**Luke 12:34** – *"For where your treasure is, there your heart will be also".* (NKJV)

My hidden idol in life was my husband. I would do anything for him and invested all my time and energy into trying to make him happy because he was always so hurt and unhappy. I didn't realize this truth until our separation, and it was hard to acknowledge. I felt like my life would literally end without him and I often prayed it would.

He was my whole life even though he never really believed it. Believe me when I say to you God is a jealous God, and He desires to be first in your life. If you let something or someone else come before God, you are very likely to lose that thing that you value so much.

Spend some time to analyze where God fits in your life. Is He at the center or is He an afterthought? If he is an afterthought, what can you do today to make God your focus? It doesn't have to be some drastic measure. Start with small goals, like reading your Bible for fifteen minutes a day, reading a devotional every day, listening to a Christian radio station, substituting TV time for God time, going to church, joining a Bible study group, or spending more time in prayer. It may take baby steps at first, but you will find it easier to make God the priority in your life and begin to find other ways to spend time with God daily.

## Worry is a Waste of Time

**Matthew 6:27** – *Who of you by worrying can add a single hour to his life?* (NIV)

**Philippians 4:6** – *Be anxious for nothing, but in everything by prayer and supplication, with thanksgiving, let your requests be made known to God.* (NKJV)

Control is an illusion. We are not in control of life, other people or their feelings, our circumstances, our spouse, our children, or even our vehicle. The only thing we can control (and even that is difficult) is our emotions, our decisions, our thoughts, and our actions. God is in control. So, when things feel out of control, turn those things over to God whether it be your circumstance, difficult situation, relationships, your loved ones, your pain, or whatever it is. Give it to God. There is no situation that is greater than our God!

**Matthew 6:34** – *Therefore do not worry about tomorrow, for tomorrow will worry about its own things. Sufficient for the day is its own trouble.* (NKJV)

**1 Peter 5:7** – *Cast all of your anxiety on Him because He cares for you.* (NIV)

My mom was a big worrier and unfortunately so

was I. I was a very rule based person and had a strong sense of responsibility. I always considered the risks in the choices I made, and I wouldn't risk more than I was willing to or could afford to lose. I was fearful of so many things and lived life anxiously. The older I became and the stronger my faith became in the Lord, the less I worried about things. God helped me to realize that there was so much of my life that was out of my control and I had to just trust Him and continue to go to Him in prayer to meet my needs.

I had often done things in my life where others would say "I don't know how you do it". Most of the time, I wasn't really thinking about how I would accomplish all that needed to be done. I just leaned on God and knew that He would help me through. I never doubted that God would make a way. Even in my marriage. I have had to realize that regardless of how hard I pray and do my part, things sometimes still go wrong. But even when they do, God is there to help us through. He knows best and will show us the way through the storm.

**Psalm 68:19** – *Praise be to the Lord, to God our Savior, who daily bears our burdens.* (NIV)

## Turn Your Test Into Your Testimony

Shakespeare was right…. life really is a tragedy but sometimes it's a tragic comedy. Life is hard and sometimes life is REALLY HARD. There is no easy button in life. If there was, you would probably discover it was a dead end and have to come back to the beginning to start all over again.

I often felt like I was playing a game of Chutes and Ladders where there was nothing but slides and no ladders in my life. Every time I would seem to be making headway, I would suddenly be rushing back down to where I started from. But guess what? No one ever said life was going to be easy and if they did, they were lying.

Even Jesus said that life would be hard and He never lies; but He also offers hope. Do you realize that Jesus knew how rough life was and still chose to live it for us, so that we may have life eternal? He knew what He would be facing from the humble birth, fleeing for His life as an infant, the criticism, the betrayals, the lashes, the nails and the death on the cross. He knew it all and still chose to sacrifice His very life for us.

**Philippians 2:8** – *And being found in appearance as a man, He humbled Himself and became obedient to the point of death, even the death of the cross.* (NKJV)

We are going to have troubles in life, but we need to find a way to grow through those times. When we take what the Enemy meant for our harm and turn it into our testimony, we strike a mighty blow against him.

By sharing our testimony, it not only takes power away from the Enemy but it brings encouragement to others who are struggling with their own battles and glorifies and honors the Lord. Be willing to share your stories of overcoming, of surviving the storms of life, and of the victories you have received in Jesus and you will see chains break that were holding you down. Draw closer to the Lord and you will begin to float in the storms of life instead of struggling against the waves in your own strength, wearing yourself out in the process.

**John 16:33** – *"These things I have spoken to you, that in Me you may have peace. In the world you will have tribulation, but be of good cheer, I have overcome the world."* (NKJV)

# Where There Is God, There Is a Way

**Psalm 91** – *¹He who dwells in the shelter of the Most High will rest in the shadow of the Almighty. ²I will say of the Lord, "He is my refuge and my fortress; My God in whom I trust". ³Surely He will save you from the fowler's snare and from the deadly pestilence. ⁴He will cover you with His feathers, and under His wings you will find refuge; His faithfulness will be your shield and rampart. ⁵You will not fear the terror of night, nor the arrow that flies by day, ⁶nor the pestilence that stalks in the darkness, nor the plague that destroys at midday. ⁷A thousand may fall at your side, ten thousand at your right hand, but it will not come near you. ⁸You will only observe with your eyes and see the punishment of the wicked. ⁹If you make the Most High your dwelling – even the Lord, who is my refuge – ¹⁰then no harm will overtake you, no disaster will come near your tent.*

*¹¹For He will command His angels concerning you to guard you in all your ways; ¹²they will lift you up in their hands, so that you will not strike your foot against a stone. ¹³You will tread on the lion and the cobra; you will trample the great lion and the serpent. ¹⁴"Because He loves Me," says the Lord, "I will rescue him; I will protect him, for he acknowledges My name. ¹⁵He will call upon Me and I will answer him; I will be with him in trouble, I will deliver him and honor him. ¹⁶With long life will I satisfy him and show him my salvation".* (NIV)

God is infinite. This means that the things of God are infinite. He has infinite grace, mercy, love and abilities. God provides the grace sufficient for us to face this day and each morning He provides a fresh anointing of grace for that day. He wants us to live our lives through faith that He will carry us through whatever comes our way.

Too often we are like the Israelites trying to store up the manna for tomorrow, but God knows just what we need and will provide for those needs. Leave tomorrow's concerns for tomorrow and live for today. This does not mean to live irresponsibly. We should still be aware of how the choices and decisions we make today will affect tomorrow, but don't carry the burden of your tomorrows before they come.

**Psalm 23:1** – *The Lord is my shepherd; I shall not want.* (KJV)

**Philippians 4:19** – *And my God shall supply all your need according to His riches in glory by Christ Jesus.* (NKJV)

No matter what storm or fire you are facing; have faith that you are not facing it alone and God is a good, good Father. Regardless of the reason you are facing the storms of life, remember that God is on your side and there is no one and nothing greater than He. Thank and praise Him through it all because you KNOW He will bring you through it.

There are times when you will feel like giving up; when you just get over one crashing wave and another one comes slamming down over you, submerging you beneath the deep waters again. But in those darkest times, when you feel the most alone, find peace and comfort in the fact that God has your hand held tightly in His and He will not let go. Even if you don't feel Him there, I promise He is.

**Ephesians 6:13-17** – *[13]Therefore put on the full armor of God, so that when the day of evil comes, you may be able to stand your ground and after you have done everything, to stand. [14]Stand firm then, with the belt of truth buckled around your waist, with the breastplate of righteousness in place, [15]and with your feet fitted with the readiness that comes from the gospel of peace. [16]In addition to all this, take up the shield of faith, with which you can extinguish all the flaming arrows of the evil one. [17]Take the helmet of salvation and the sword of the Spirit, which is the word of God.* (NIV)

Trust in Him. He will get you through. Put on the full armor of God and let Him be your great defender. It is not an earthly battle that we face but the continual onslaught of the Enemy, and we are only equipped to face him by God.

**Psalm 18:35** – *You have also given me the shield of Your salvation, Your right hand has held me up, Your gentleness has made me great.* (NKJV)

There will also be times when you want to go for the jugular of the one who has hurt you. Give them grace and forgive them whenever it is possible, because God is our defender and He will know our hearts in the end. Pray for your enemies and love those who persecute you.

Jesus was hated and persecuted all the way to the cross and He still said, "Father, forgive them, for they do not know what they do" (**Luke 23:34**). We are all broken people and if Christ gave His life for me how can I do any less for others? I will do my best to forgive them.

Unforgiveness shackles you to them and often harms you more than the one who injured you in the first place. It isn't always easy and it is against our human nature, but forgive where it is in your power to do so and pray to God to help you forgive when it is not. Walk in peace with God as much as you can and you will make it through the storms.

**Proverbs 21:2** – *Every way of a man is right in his own eyes, but the Lord weighs the hearts.* (NKJV)

**Romans 12:19** – *Beloved, do not avenge yourselves, but rather give place to wrath; for it is written, "Vengeance is Mine, I will repay," says the Lord.* (NKJV)

**Psalm 66:12** – *You let men ride over our heads; we went through fire and water, but you brought us to a place of abundance.* (NIV)

**1 John 5:4** – *For whatever is born of God overcomes the world. And this is the victory that has overcome the world – our faith.* (NKJV)

# Always Forward

**Philippians 3:12-** *Not that I have already obtained this, or have already been made perfect, but I press on to take hold of that for which Christ Jesus took hold of me.* (NIV)

Always forward was something my father-in-law would always say. It became a motto to our family. It was even the greeting when entering one of the bases where my husband was stationed.

"Always forward" really resonates with me especially in times of crisis in my life when I am facing the deadliest storms and most intense fires. Webster defines forward as "moving, tending or leading toward a position in front", ready, belonging at the front, "of, relating to, or getting ready for the future", and "notably advanced or developed". To me, it represents the fact that I can never go back, I have to keep moving forward (even if it is at a snail's pace), regardless of how I may feel or my desires to just give up and fall into a crumbling mass of tears and self-pity.

God calls us to walk forward in faith in spite of our circumstances, our own desires, the obstacles we face or the lies of the Enemy. When we walk forward in faith, He will guide our steps, taking us by the hand and leading us forward by the Spirit within us.

Take up your cross and follow Christ and live as Christ-like a life as you possibly can; keep your focus on God, continuously seeking His face; moving forward by the leading of the Holy Spirit in your life and you will make it through the stormy fires and tribulations you are facing in this life. Remember always that this life is temporary but there is an eternal reward for God's children.

**Exodus 14:15** – *And the Lord said to Moses, "Why do you cry to me? Tell the children of Israel to go forward." (NKJV)*

**Proverbs 4:25** – *Let your eyes look straight ahead, and fix your gaze directly before you.* (NIV)

**Proverbs 16:9** – *A man's heart plans his way, but the Lord directs his steps.* (NKJV)

**Ezekiel 1:12** – *And each one went straight forward; they went wherever the spirit wanted to go, and they did not turn when they went.* (NKJV)

## Conclusion

My dear brothers and sisters in Christ, I pray that God will guide you through the storms you face in this life, that He will safeguard and keep you, and that you will put on the full armor of God that it will protect you from the attacks of the Enemy that you will surely face in this life.

I am still walking through the fire and raging storm in my own life, but I trust in the Lord to be my defender and my place of refuge when I grow weary from the walk. I stand upon the promises of His word that I will be a victor and not a victim in this life because He who is within me is greater than he who is in the world.

My hope is in God through Christ and the Holy Spirit. I choose to walk with them daily, seeking to know them better and better each day. I choose to grow where I am planted and tend my garden to remove any weeds and pests that are trying to take over and destroy the good fruit that is growing there. I choose to not grow stagnant in the waiting but to fill my Spirit continuously with the Word and God's leading.

I pray that you will do the same. I sincerely hope

that by sharing my journey and my testimony, it brought you some peace and at least the knowledge that you are not alone. We all struggle in this life and it is okay to not be okay and to seek encouragement and strength from others. I encourage you to share your testimony with others and to find the resources you need through Godly wisdom from fellow brothers and sisters in Christ, fellowship in small groups, and by meeting with the Lord daily.

If you are not already, I strongly encourage you to get into church and get into the Word. I promise you it saved my life. I wouldn't be here writing this story without it.

May all the blessing of the Father pour out upon you and may He turn the tides of the storms raging against you. – In Jesus's Holy Name, Amen.

**Isaiah 43:2** – *When you pass through the waters, I will be with you; and through the rivers, they shall not overflow you. When you walk through the fire, you shall not be burned, nor shall the flame scorch you.* (NKJV).

**Romans 5:3-4** – *³And not only that, but we also glory in tribulations, knowing that tribulation produces perseverance; ⁴and perseverance, character; and character, hope.* (NKJV)